Nostalgic
BURY

The publishers would like to thank the following companies for their

support in the production of this book

Main sponsor
Tetrosyl

Antler Ltd

Bury College

Bury Van Group

Holy Cross College

McKenzie-Martin

Printpack

Radcliffe Glass & Windows

Senior Hargreaves

D.G. Steel & Son Engineering Ltd

Wallwork Heat Treatment

J&W Whewell Ltd

First published in Great Britain by True North Books Limited
England HX3 6SN
01422 244555
www.truenorthbooks.com

ISBN 978 - 1906649722

Text, design and origination by True North Books
Printed and bound by The Amadeus Press

Nostalgic
BURY

CONTENTS

INTRODUCTION

Such has been the popularity of our previous books on the Bury area, that we have been encouraged to produce a new publication. Our books allow readers to walk on cobbled streets, browse in well known local shops of the period and revisit special events and occasions, without leaving the comfort of their favourite armchair. 'Change' is relentless and in some parts of the area the transformation will be more obvious than others.

Bury centre and the roads around it have changed significantly from times gone by. Some of the older and architecturally impressive buildings have retained their originality on the outside, however, their uses have changed. The title of this new book, 'Nostalgic Bury', tells you all you need to know about what is captured within its pages.

Turning over leaf after leaf will bring you to a treasure trove from the last century. Through the photographs, images and thoughtful text, the reader is taken on a steam train ride back through the mists of time to an age when dad could buy a suit at the Fifty Shilling Tailor and mum used to divvy-up at the Co-op. We make no

apologies for the fact that some of the photographs will be outside living memory because they will still be familiar to us. They may feature an event described to us by a close relative or they could feature historical landmarks such as bridges and buildings.

Whatever the view taken on the boundaries which separate 'history', 'nostalgia' or 'the present', we should all invest a little time occasionally to reflect on the past and the people and events which helped to shape life as we know it today. The last hundred years have witnessed a consolidation of the town as a commercial and retail centre. The more recent growth of the town has retained its historic core, now included in the Conservation Area with many listed buildings.

Bury has always been a vibrant town, buzzing with energy, but different episodes in its life can be seen here. So, think of youthful days paddling in the lido or courting in the cinemas of old and be entertained again as we revisit Nostalgic Bury…happy memories!

FORWARD IN UNITY

TEXT	STEVE AINSWORTH, BRENDAN O'NEILL
PHOTOGRAPH RESEARCH	BRENDAN O'NEILL
DESIGNER	SEAMUS MOLLOY
BUSINESS DEVELOPMENT MANAGER	PETER PREST

STREET SCENES

Above: Here's Bolton Street pictured in the early 1900s. Cobbled roadway and tram tracks identify the period just as much as the clothes worn by the young pedestrians looking towards the cameraman. The oh-so fashionable lady on the advertising hoarding is dressed in what will very soon be Edwardian rather than late-Victorian clothing and she is advertising the high profile shop of Robinson's in Water Street. In the bottom right hand corner is an advertisement for Nestles Milk. Nestlé originated in a 1905 merger of the Anglo-Swiss Milk Company and Farine Lactée Henri Nestlé. The company grew significantly during the First World War and again following the Second World War, eventually expanding its offerings beyond its early condensed milk and infant formula products.

Below: A fabulous picture from the turn of the last century showing the world famous Bury Market and Market Theatre. Market trading was one of the earliest recorded commercial activities in Bury, as it was in most traditional English towns. The market building pictured here was opened in 1901 at a cost of £15,000 by the Mayor Cllr John Battersby. A year earlier, traders had been given notice to quit at the previous facility in Kay Gardens because the glass roof of the building was declared unsafe. How many readers can recall a visit to the Market Theatre? The memories of long gone Christmas pantos surely never fade. In the days before television, before radio, even before cinema live entertainment was the order of the day. Theatres and variety halls proliferated all over Britain and folk flocked to them in numbers unimaginable today. Live entertainment was available everywhere, not least in pubs when before the advent of the juke box a piano player was a must, an essential accompaniment to the karaoke of the day in a time when nearly everyone could do a turn of some sort. Meanwhile, at the theatre a few pennies to sit in 'the gods' could transport one from the everyday world to a magical kingdom, if only for an hour or two.

Did you know?

The Romans are believed to have arrived in Bury around 78 AD

Right: The two little urchins pictured in Brandlesholme in the early 20th century remind us that times were hard in the olden days. One of the little mites seems to be using a chair back as a toy – no gameboys, cowboy outfits or bicycles back then. And just the dirt outside the front door to play in. 'Ah, but you were lucky' as the famous Monty Python sketch went back in the late 1960s. In truth these toddlers really are lucky, at least they have boots on their feet – though not neceassrily new to them. Incredible as it seems now in the 21st century the poorest children in Bury a hundred years ago often went about barefoot. And not just in Bury it was a national phenomenon. So widespread was the problem that a national charity existed just to provide poor children with boots.

Below: Bolton Street a hundred years ago offers a perfect picture of times gone by. A gas lamp, of course. Cloth caps, naturally. And clogs, what else? Cobbled streets and dirt were once the daily lot of everyone in Bury. The world was not just black and white back then because that is how we see it in photographs: the world really was much more black than it is today. Coal fires in homes, and factory chimneys spewing out smoke all day, meant that everything was covered in soot. Clothes left out to dry on the line soon got smut on them to the everlasting annoyance of housewives. Almost as quickly new

buildings acquired a deep patina of dirt, so much so that stone buildings soon began to look a though that had actually been built of black stone.

Above: Walmersley Road, Bury, one fine summer around midday in the first quarter of the 20th century. Astonishingly, there is not a single vehicle to be seen. No motorcars, and no trams. There is, however, clear evidence that at least one horse-drawn vehicle has gone by in the not too distant past. On the right is a very smartly turned out young man in the latest style – well at least the latest style thought appropriate for boys of his age. Eton collars and knickerbockers may have been popular with better off parents but they were not so popular with their offspring. Whilst their elders may have nodded approvingly the outfits were more likely to draw guffaws of derision from the boys' peers.

Left: Hollins Lane takes its name from the holly trees that once grew there. The holly was grown to provide winter food for cattle. By the early years of the 20th century the holly and the cattle had long since gone to be replaced by houses. In the pre-motorcar age children could happily play in the road: the only vehicles likely to appear would be pulled by a horse, whose speed would be just a few miles per hour, plenty of time to get away, and the clip clop of hooves on the cobbles would give everyone plenty of warning. The gas lights lining the street provided plenty of opportunity for night time games too – something not available to earlier generations.

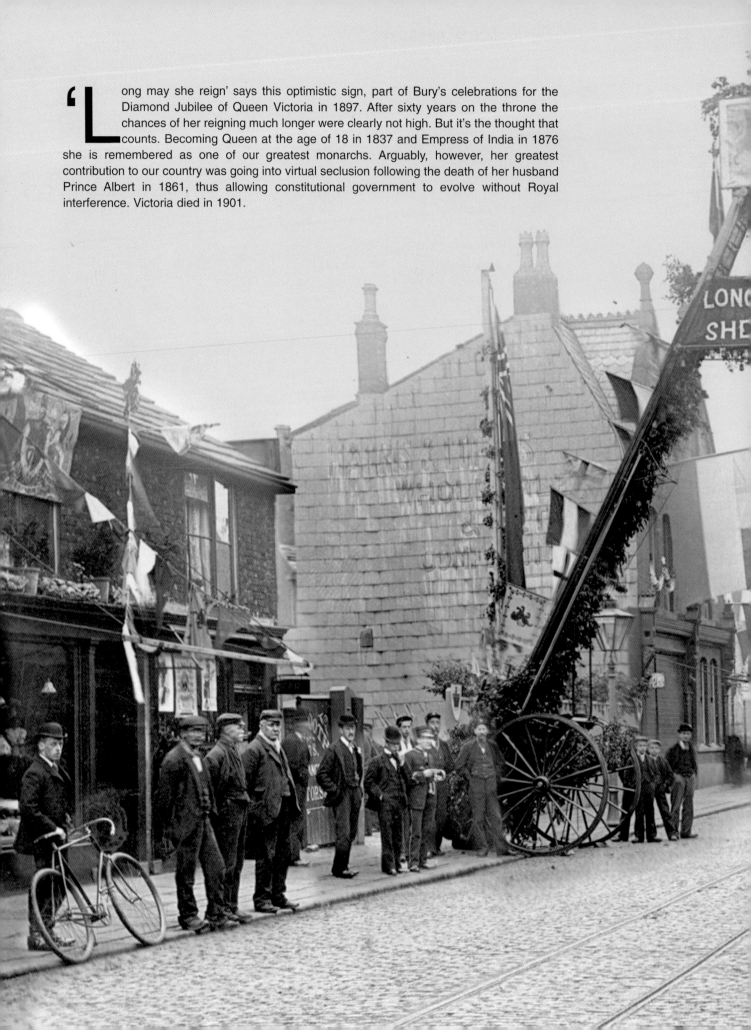

'Long may she reign' says this optimistic sign, part of Bury's celebrations for the Diamond Jubilee of Queen Victoria in 1897. After sixty years on the throne the chances of her reigning much longer were clearly not high. But it's the thought that counts. Becoming Queen at the age of 18 in 1837 and Empress of India in 1876 she is remembered as one of our greatest monarchs. Arguably, however, her greatest contribution to our country was going into virtual seclusion following the death of her husband Prince Albert in 1861, thus allowing constitutional government to evolve without Royal interference. Victoria died in 1901.

Above: The Parish Church is of medieval origin and is located at the highest point in the town centre. A church has existed on this site since 1189. There was a substantial rebuilding in 1776. The detached west broach spire is of 1844-5 and the remaining parts of the church are a result of a further rebuilding by Crowther of 1871-6. The nave stands 76ft 6ins high, 84ft 6ins long and 30ft wide,

the two were joined by the addition of a narthex. The windows on the north wall depict Old Testament figures whilst the south windows are of New Testament figures. The churchyard is largely paved with gravestones which pre date the current building. The rear of the church provides views of Holcombe Moor and Peel Tower. The town's war memorial is found on the south-west corner of the church's site. The Market Place consists of impressive sandstone facades of mid 19th century commercial properties built in a predominantly Classical style. The quality of the enclosing buildings are an indication of the prosperity of the town during that period. In this area during the mid 17th century a market cross stood at the centre of the triangular market place whilst a pillory and stocks were further to the east. The statue and monument by E. H. Bailey is to Sir Robert Peel, born at Chamber Hall, in Bury, in 1788, is sited directly in front of the church. The store to the left is Driffield Brothers, well known outfitters of the time.

Bottom left: Bury has had a market since 1444. And here is a shot of Market Street just before the First World War. The scene is an unusually quiet one, either the photographer was up very early in the morning, or perhaps it's a Sunday and everyone is having a lie-in. The street lights featured here are wonderful examples of electric lighting which would eventually supersede gas street lights. No expense seems to have been spared to produce these prestigious works of art – a far

cry from our modern utilitarian approach to 'street furniture'. Parked at the side of the street is a large handcart: in those long gone days not everyone could afford a pony and those lower down the economic scale frequently hitched their means of transport to 'shanks pony' instead of a four-legged one.

Did you know?

The market town was first mentioned as a parish in AD 962

Below: Here's Fleet Street in 1900. No, not that other Fleet Street in London once home to most national newspapers, but our Fleet Street in Bury. There is not a car in sight, though no doubt there were a few in the town. Horses are still the order of the day. Rather surprisingly for a town centre the road bed still appears to be unmetalled. Cobbles or stone setts were normal in urban streets; yet Fleet Street looks not to have been paved. And Tarmacadam would not be patented for another year. Generally, until the middle of the century, and certainly in the countryside, many roads were simply made up of a bed of crushed rocks, a road-building system that had been introduced on the toll roads of the 18th century. They were fine for horses and carts. But once motor cars got on them the result was vast potholes and huge clouds of dust.

Above: Here's Stoney Brow, Tottington, captured on a sunny day long before the motor car changed our lives. Open fields and trees can be seen in the distance enhancing Tottington's place as a rural backwater rather than a commuter town. A horse and cart emerges from Crowther Street, although today we would see this as Turton Road. The houses to the left where the three gentlemen are standing, are no longer there, as the road meanders off down Harwood Road towards Bolton. To the right on Chapel Street, Crowther's Pure Ales and Dunvilles VR Old Irish Whiskey are being promoted on the side of the pub and on its windows. Labour in those days really was thirsty work; manual work with few labour saving devices drove many men to the pub even before they went home for their tea. In recent times this building would probably be better known to locals as Carmelo's Italian restaurant.

Below: Historically a part of Lancashire, Tottington's early history is marked by its status as an important Medieval fee, a type of Royal Manor which encompassed several townships. This Royal Manor of Tottington stretched from Musbury and Cowpe with Lench in the north to Affetside in the west and Walshaw in the south west. This photograph of Market Street might almost have been taken in medieval times by the look of the buildings. Only the telegraph pole in the distance gives the game away – and the aptly named Weekly Telegraph, and Woman's Life advertised on the boards on the right. One hopes the teas and suppers being advertised were more appetising than the building.

Above: The name Greenmount came into existence in 1848 when the Sunday School was built. It was originally spelt Green Mount. Some residents of the older generation, who were born in Greenmount, still write it as two separate words. Greenmount was, in 1848, part of the outskirts of the village of Tottington. At first, people who lived near to the Sunday School included the name of Greenmount in their address and gradually this was extended to the surrounding area and so Greenmount became a village. Prominent in this Edwardian photograph is Greenmount United Reform Church in Holcombe Road. Whether or not vandals have been at play is uncertain, though the gas lamp missing its top suggests that the youngster playing in the road may not be quite as innocent as they look.

Bottom left: By1936 loading tramcars in the middle of the road, at the junction of two major trunk roads - the A56 Chester to Skipton and the A58 Liverpool to Hull roads - was becoming a perilous practice. However, it was to continued until 1948 when, following the closure of the Tottington Route, the Walmersley Terminus was moved into Market Street.

Below: No you are not seeing things, this man is actually waiting at the bus terminus at Kay Gardens, for a bus to Jericho. Not however, the longest bus journey ever to the West Bank in Palestine, but a couple of miles East of Bury along the Rochdale Old Road. The No 23 bus in front is waiting to set off in the opposite direction, on the 7 mile journey to Bolton. Kay Gardens was the terminus for all bus services from surrounding districts and towns.

Right: The idea of erecting a large clock tower in the centre of Bury originated with Henry Whitehead who wished to provide a suitable memorial for his recently deceased brother, Walter Whitehead (1840-1913). The site agreed upon was a triangular-shaped piece of land between Knowsley Street and Manchester Road, which had once been occupied by a lunatic asylum. The architects, Maxwell and Tuke, who had long connections with Bury, were responsible for designing the clock tower in a style which they classified as 'Old English of the late Tudor period.' By the New Year the contractors, F. M. and H. Nuttall of Whitefield, were preparing the foundations. By the early summer the Shropshire clockmakers, J. B. Joyce were installing the clock. The Whitehead memorial clock tower and gardens were opened by Sir Frederick Treves in June 1914. The Whitehead Clock Tower Gardens are pictured here in 1972. The particular event being recorded for posterity is the Golden Jubilee of the St John Ambulance Cadets whose symbol is so clearly visible in the foreground. St John Ambulance Cadets is the youth section of St John Ambulance for members aged between 10 and 17. It was founded in 1922 to train young people in first aid and other essential skills and has grown to be one of the biggest youth organisations in the UK, with over 20,000 members.

D ownhams sits well in the centre of this view of The Rock with Union Street entering from the right. The prominent building had been home to the well-know iron mongers for many years. It was founded in the 1850s, a century before this picture was taken in 1958. The owners may well have used the bank on the opposite corner, William Deacons, for their business transactions and it would be nice to think they looked at their finest after being 'suited and booted' at Alexander's and Van Allan's just next door. This fine building was sadly demolished in 1971 to make way for further pedestrianisation.

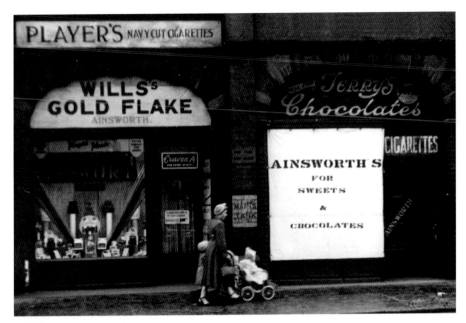

Does anywhere still sell 'thick twist' we wonder – those ropes of pipe tobacco, black as liquorice, sold curled up in tins. Is there an old men's parliament anywhere in which elderly men still cut their 'baccy' off the rope and rub it between their palms to prepare it for smoking? Sadly, perhaps not.

Above: Ainsworth is one of the Bury area's oldest surnames. It's also one of the commonest. Every Ainsworth in Bury must have had an ancestor who once travelled the short distance from the next door settlement of Ainsworth. Here in 1950 is S Ainsworth's tobacconists and sweet shop. Sweet shops may still be around, but there are very few tobacconists to be seen these days. Once there were any number of shops specialising in selling cigarettes, cigars, snuff, pipe tobacco and pipes, not to mention lighters, matches, pipe cleaners and those useful silver penknives for reaming out and tamping down.

Below: Today it is hard to grasp just how important the Co-op and its famous annual 'divvy' once were. The Rochdale Society of Equitable Pioneers was a group of 28 weavers and other artisans formed in 1844. They decided to band together to open their own store selling food items they could not otherwise afford. They designed the famous Rochdale Principles. They collected one pound per person for a total of 28 pounds of capital. On 21 December, 1844, they opened their store with a meagre selection of butter, sugar, flour, oatmeal and a few candles. Within three months they had expanded their selection to include tea and tobacco. A decade later, the co-operative movement had grown to nearly 1,000 co-operatives. By the time this photo was taken in Bury the Co-op had long been a local and national institution. Flanking Kay Gardens, it was a department store which also housed a restaurant on the first floor widely used by office workers at lunch times, and of course for funeral parties.

Below: It's interesting to see the old ambulance on Market Place in 1963 just about to pass the Westminster Bank. On its left we can see a line of several fine cars which must be carrying visiting dignitaries to Bury Town Hall. Sir Robert Peel overlooks the scene from his prominent position on the left of the picture. His statue was erected in 1852 at a cost of £2,500 and was unveiled two years after the death of Bury's most famous son, by Frederick Peel MP. Robert Peel was born at Chamber Hall in 1788, the eldest son of a wealthy cotton manufacturer. He was educated at Harrow and Oxford and became Home Secretary in 1822, creating the Metropolitan Police Force. He served twice as prime minister, 1835-35 and 1841-46, and is remembered for repealing the Corn Laws and his liberalism towards Catholic emancipation, neither of which sat well with the wealthy landowners and staunch Protestants. Peel Tower on Holcombe Hill was erected the day after this statue was unveiled.

Right: If we look beyond the lady cyclist in this 1964 photo we can see Downham's ironmongers in the distance and behind the trees to the left No. 1 The Rock, a Tudor-fronted building known as Union Buildings. A strange name for a central street in a northern town, The Rock was named in 1935 and ran from St Mary's Church to Moorgate previously taking in Fleet Street, Rock Street, Stanley Street and Water Street. The Westminster Bank stands proudly on the corner to the right of the picture.

Above: The unusually named Pineapple Inn, situated on Union Street, was one of Bury Brewery's more popular hostelries in the town. The highly polished Morris and Humber cars show what will have been a great personal pride of the owners of these vehicles at the time, parking their prized possessions in the centre of town. This scene in 1963 seems a long way from the momentous events taking place elsewhere. It was the year of the Great Train Robbery when daring thieves stole £1million from a Post Office mail train.

Right: The old Fire Station in the Rock, pictured here in 1965, was later replaced by a modern building, the future of which is also now under threat of redevelopment. When built the old fire station was itself a state-of-the-art facility. A major change in the way fires were fought came into being in the mid 1850s when the first reliable steam powered appliances were adopted by brigades. These appliances replaced the manual engines and allowed a far greater quantity of water to be to be directed onto a fire. Those steam-powered appliances were only to last slightly longer than 50 years due to the introduction of the internal combustion engine in the early 1900s. Before 1938 there were between 1,400 and 1,500 small municipal fire brigades run by local councils in the UK.

Left: The Market Place in Bury has seen many changes down the centuries. At first glance this picture taken in 1965 shows a very modern scene. Closer inspection, however, reveals much that has changed, especially the traffic: there are not many Reliant three-wheelers about these days. And the buses don't have open platforms at the back: they mostly disappeared in the early 1970s to be replaced by less draughty vehicles. The AEC Routemaster is a model of double-decker bus that was built by Associated Equipment Company (AEC) and in production until 1968. Primarily front-engined, rear open-platform buses, a small number of variants were produced with doors and/or front entrances. Introduced by London Transport in 1956. The Routemaster survived in London until 2005.

Above: Georgiana Street and the old Market Hall in Bury in 1968 is bustling on this fine sunny day – one just hopes that the cameraman was quick enough to jump out of the way of the car which appears to be about to run him down. Bury was changing rapidly when this scene was captured. In the post-war period, there was a major decline in the cotton industry, and in common with many Lancashire towns, Bury's skyline was soon very different than it had been, with countless factory chimneys being pulled down and many mills closing their doors forever. Elsewhere, the old shopping area around Princess Street and Union Square, for example, was being demolished and a concrete precinct emerged to replace it.

Below Further down Georgiana Street these three youngster look to have just enjoyed a yummy cornet treat from Sorrento Ices. One guesses a few minutes earlier the sound of footsteps were heard coming through the door at pace followed by the words "mum, mum, can i have an ice-cream, awe please mum, please...thanks mum."

Above: Back in August 1970 when this photo was taken Beryl Howarth was staring out across the wasteland of old prams, bricks and broken bottles outside her home in Ferngrove. The housing estate would be sliced in two by a new by-pass. The first motorway had been the Preston by-pass, which had opened in 1958. The M62 was built from 1971 to 1976. In 1949 a report, the Road Plan for Lancashire, proposed the construction of Route 9 which would link north east Manchester with Burnley and Blackburn. Originally planned to be an all purpose road, the route was redesignated as a motorway, the M66, prior to construction. The first section (the so called Middleton Link) was opened in 1971. Construction then began on the southern section of the Bury bypass in February 1973 and this opening in August 1975.

Right: Much of old Bury disappeared in the 1960s and 1970s in a wave of enthusiasm for 'progress' and all things modern. Some folk at least saw the need to make a record of what was being lost. Here is Rochdale Old Road where local historians are taking pictures of a part of old Bury before it is too late and the demolition men turn yet another street to rubble. The weavers' cottages on Rochdale Old Road needed to come down to

make way for a road widening scheme. The long windows of the upper storeys clearly show that they once were the workshops of handloom weavers who needed all the light they could get. An attempt to demolish a similar building today would cause public outrage.

Above: A gigantic image of a Spitfire adorns the gable end of Hornby Street adorns this unusual picture. The artwork was part of a big cleanup of the area, and was painted by local artists Walter Kershaw, from Rochdale, and Eric Kean, from Bury, in January 1973. Eric Kean, who died in 2008, was born in Heywood in 1930. During the 1950s he began working as a television engineer but continued to paint in his spare time. Later Eric joined classes at the Bury School of Arts and Crafts. In the 1970s he joined forces with fellow artist Walter Kershaw. Their endeavours together included painting bridges and large scale murals in Bury, Heywood, Rochdale and Manchester. They were among the first graffiti artists but with great artistic flare. Some of their most notable subjects were this Spitfire, steam trains and a large scale portrait of singer Alvin Stardust.

Right: It's January 1976 and Emma Rice, aged five, is pictured admiring the stone lions at the entrance to Bury Lions public garden in Crompton Street. Emma is modelling that still-popular item of winter clothing the duffle coat. The duffle coat owes its popularity to the British Royal Navy, which issued a camel-coloured variant of it as an item of warm clothing during World War One. The design of the coat was modified slightly and widely issued during the Second World War. In the Navy, it was referred to as a 'convoy coat'. Large stocks of post-war military surplus coats made available at reasonable prices to the general public meant that these coats became a ubiquitous and popular item of clothing, most especially in the 1950s and 1960s.

Left: Bury Parish Church of St Mary the Virgin which dominates this picture of the Market Place is located at the highest point in the town centre. Although the present building is Victorian there has been a church on the site for over 1,000 years; in medieval times the west door would have looked out across the market place to the castle. The steeple pre-dates the church, having been built in 1842. The church was designed a few years later by J S Crowther on a much grander scale. The present church was consecrated on 2 February, 1876, having taken five years to build. The church was the garrison church for the Lancashire Fusiliers and colours of the Regiment hang proudly from their pikes around the walls of the nave.

Bottom left: What an evocative photograph of the back of Walmersley Road in Bury taken in 1977. Coronation Street eat your heart out. This is the real deal. For a hundred years thousands of local folk were brought up in houses backing onto rear alleyways exactly like this one. Older folk will readily recall outside toilets and the complete absence of bathrooms. And we had proper dustbins, though in the days of coal fires the bins were rarely full, anything combustible went on the fire; rubbish was after all was cheaper to burn than coal. By 1977, however, the worst of the old housing had been demolished whilst the better properties had had central heating and bathrooms for many years.

> ## Did you know?
>
> *In 1838, out of 1,058 working class houses in Bury investigated by the Manchester Statistical Society, 733 had 3-4 people in each bed, 207 had 4-5 and 76 had 5-6*

Below: Knowsley Street, Bury, and the Town Hall on a fine summer's day in 1978. Happy days for motorists, with fewer than half as many cars about as there are today, and parking was seldom a problem. The Town Hall was officially opened by the Queen on the 22 October, 1954. The foundation stone had been laid some 15 years earlier, in 1939, by the Earl of Derby. The building was designed by Reginald Edmond, winner of an architectural competition. Building work actually began on site in 1938; despite the outbreak of war in 1939 work continued until 1940, by which time only the outer shell had been completed. Building work would not start again until 1947. During the war the basement was used as an air raid shelter. Today the building is the home of the Borough Council and also features the Elizabethan Suite, which is used for official and social functions.

Below: More than three decades may have passed since this photo was taken in 1978 but superficially not much has changed in Haymarket Street. The Knowsley Hotel still stands, a busy pub in the centre of Bury which is very well run and very comfortable according to those who enjoy a pint or two there. Not everything is as it was, however. The Whitbread brewery sign on the outside wall has been replaced by a large sign reading simply 'Knowsley'. Inside, Whitbread beers are gone too. The pub is now part of the Green King chain. Street signs and other 'street furniture' are rather more prolific today. And one thing on the outside of building today, and not seen in 1978, is a television satellite dish.

Above: Kay Gardens was the site of the first indoor market built by Lord Derby in 1839. This site became derelict after a new market opened in 1901, but in 1903 it was agreed to lay out the gardens in memory of the man who brought the world the flying shuttle. The memorial to John Kay was erected by noted sculptor, W.Venn Gough of Bristol, in 1908. John Kay was born, aptly, at Park, just north of Bury, on 17 June, 1704. The youngster was apprenticed to a reed maker - reeds are comb-like devices attached to hand loom that keep the warp threads separated. Kay showed the first hint of his creative genius when he designed a replacement for reeds made from polished wire.

But, by 1730, he was in Bury where he patented a machine for twisting and cording mohair and worsted. Then, three years later, he revealed to the world his flying shuttle - the invention that arguably was to do more than any other to kick start the Industrial Revolution. In this picture the photographer has captured a very open view across Kay Gardens, with building work taking place in the background and to the right, a bus waiting in Haymarket Street. Many features shown here combine to rekindle fond memories of the way the area used to look, before the age of pedestrianisation. Today, the view would be much more built up and enclosed.

ENTERTAINMENT
LEISURE & PASTIMES

Below: Bury's late-Victorian Art Gallery, Museum and Archives re-opened on 13 May, 2005 following a £1.2 million refit. A visible sign of the town's prosperity following the Industrial Revolution the original institution opened its doors in 1901 to house Thomas Wrigley's collection of Victorian art, given to the town by his family in celebration of Queen Victoria's Diamond Jubilee. The Gallery is something of a work of art in itself, with fine mosaic floors and stained glass windows. The Museum is known as Paradise Street, laid out with shops and room settings. Family-friendly activities are always available, with extra events at holiday time. The lively programme of changing exhibitions is accompanied by talks and workshops.

Left: This is the 1896 Bury water polo team pictured in all their Victorian glory. Men certainly knew how to grow real moustaches and beards in those days. This is of course a studio portrait and the lads have had to get changed into their 'cozzies' for the occasion. The rules of water polo were originally developed in the late nineteenth century by William Wilson the first 'Baths Master' of the Arlington Baths Club in Glasgow. The first games of 'aquatic football' were played at the Arlington in 1870. Bury County Borough Baths Committee was formed in 1876 to provide a municipal swimming bath, as well as 'slipper baths' where folk could go for a soak in a hot tub.

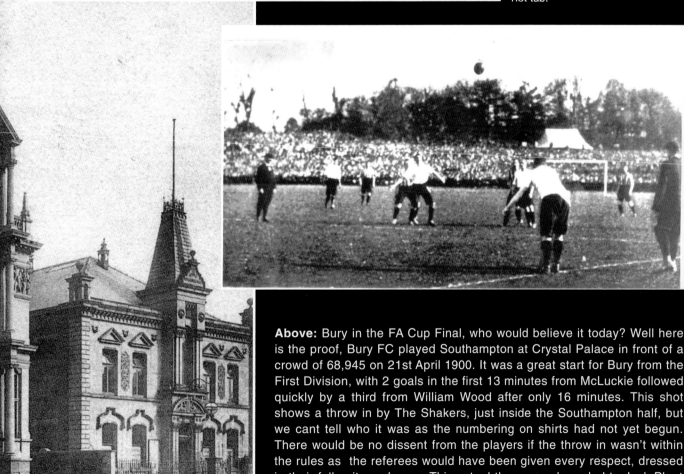

Above: Bury in the FA Cup Final, who would believe it today? Well here is the proof, Bury FC played Southampton at Crystal Palace in front of a crowd of 68,945 on 21st April 1900. It was a great start for Bury from the First Division, with 2 goals in the first 13 minutes from McLuckie followed quickly by a third from William Wood after only 16 minutes. This shot shows a throw in by The Shakers, just inside the Southampton half, but we cant tell who it was as the numbering on shirts had not yet begun. There would be no dissent from the players if the throw in wasn't within the rules as the referees would have been given every respect, dressed in their full suits and caps. This actual throw may have led to Jack Plant scoring Bury's final goal just 10 minutes from time. A great day for Bury FC and its spectators which would be repeated only 3 years later in 1903 with another Bury FA Cup win!

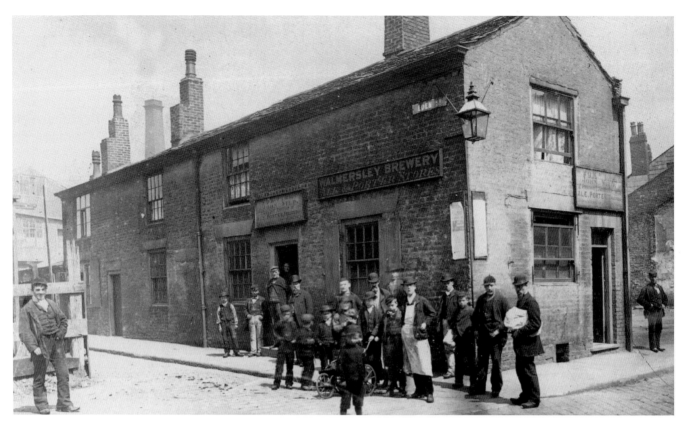

Above: Here's the long-gone Fox Inn, in Eden Street. The sign on the wall is advertising the ales of the Falmersley brewery, itself a name now also lost to Bury's beer drinking fraternity. This very early photograph captures the scene outside the pub at some time well before the First World War. The Great War changed Britain's drinking habits quite remarkably. Until then pubs could, and did, stay open all the hours they wished. And thirsty workmen in heavy manual jobs made full use of them. Concerned that drunkenness at work might damage the war effort, politicians passed the Defence of the Realm Act almost before the first shot was fired. Some of the things the public were not allowed to do included flying a kite, lighting a bonfire, buying binoculars, feeding wild animals bread, discussing naval and military matters or consuming alcohol on public transport. And alcoholic drinks were to be watered down.

gifts of land and money from a local benefactor, Mr Thomas O Openshaw. This and another three parks were opened by the Prince of Wales/Duke of Clarence, HRH Prince Albert Victor, on 21 July, 1888. The bandstand in the park was first

Above right: The Walmersley Road Recreation Ground, now known as Clarence Park, was one of four parks established following a public meeting in 1883, with contributions from Lord Derby, the Lord of the Manor, a public subscription, and, in this particular case, generous

opened on 4 November, 1899, and was presented by JP Henry Whitehead and businessman Edmund Milnes, who owned the sheet factory in Chesham. The flatness of the site was broken by a number of planted ornamental mounds designed to screen the playgrounds and cricket pitch.

Above: Who could ever think of a more fortuitous name for a garage than Carrs Ltd? This scene outside Carrs' Automobile Engineers' and taxi firm in the 1920s is very evocative as Bury day trippers get ready to set off for distant parts. The vehicles are charabancs, a name still evoked by older folk who sometimes refer to modern motor-coaches as 'Charas' or 'Sharas'. The sign on Carrs' wall reads Chara-Bancs with a hyphen: in fact there should be two hyphens. It's French. The original char-a-bancs meant a 'carriage with benches'. And indeed only a generation earlier day trippers from Bury would have been travelling in a horse drawn 'chara', and not in one of these modern motorised versions.

Right: Back in the 1920s and 1930s before homes were supplied with mains electricity, all the household chores had to be done by hand, especially the washing. On Monday morning the man of the house would be up early to light the fire and to heat the water, before the housewife would get up to prepare the wash, some items might have been left over night to 'steep'. Housewives had to hang out their washing wherever they could string up a washing line, sometimes even the back yard was not big enough and the alleyway had to be used. Here we can see newsboy Edwin Whitely, of Radcliffe, playing his mouth organ while on his rounds in May 1936. He has formed

a group with thirteen colleagues known as the Harmonica Band and he is keen to get some practice in as he delivers his papers. The harmonica's versatility brought it to the attention of classical music during the 1930s. American Larry Adler was one of the first harmonica players to perform major works. Adler taught himself harmonica (which he preferred to call a mouth-organ) and began playing professionally at the age of 14. He became widely acknowledged as one of the world's most skilled harmonica players.

Above: It's not the best start to a top fixture when you loose your goalkeeper after eight minutes with a broken knee, but that is what happened at Gigg Lane on 18 October, 1947, against Newcastle United when George Bradshaw had to be taken from the field by the St John Ambulance men. You would also think the opportunities for goals would be reduced if you then put your centre-forward in goals! But Don Carter for Bury stepped up to the challenge and supported by Bill Griffiths and Reg Halton, also seen here, Don scored a rare hat-trick. Unfortunately, the stand-in goalkeeper must have been under pressure as Newcastle were able to put five past him. The packed south stand behind this scene would have had an exciting but disappointing day as Bury lost 3-5, but an excellent crowd of 23,827 (compared to today's average of 3.436) would have boosted the Bury coffers.

Right: Gigg Lane was empty of fans on the day this photo was taken in 1965. The capacity of the ground was once 35,000 – a number reached when a record crowd

attended Bury's F.A. Cup third round tie against Bolton Wanderers on 9 January, 1960.Gigg Lane's current capacity is 11,840. The first match to be played at Gigg Lane was a friendly between Bury and Wigan Athletic on 12 September, 1885, a match which Bury won 4–3. Astonishingly, the first floodlit match to be played there took place on 5 November, 1889, before the Football League had authorised the use of floodlights in competitive matches, when a crowd of 7,000 saw Bury defeated 4–5 by Heywood Central. The stadium has had permanent floodlights since 1953. The club was formed in 1885. Gigg Lane's first ever game took place on 12 September, 1885, when Bury played a friendly match against Wigan, and won 4–3.

Above: Bury Fair was the place to be when it came to town and the big wheel in this 1960s shot preceded all the millennium wheels around UK cities we see today. The kids loved the buzz of the fair, the toffee apples which damaged growing teeth, the candy floss that gave a sticky hit of sugar. Best of all were the dodgems and waltzer. These were a real break from the normal fun of the day with footballs, conkers, skipping and rounders. What a treat to smash into your best friend's car and then race away to avoid being caught. Girls screamed as the young lads of the fair spun their cars out of control on the waltzer. Let's be frank, the fairground owners had to make money, so what if your coconut wouldn't be knocked from its perch, the metal ducks would'nt flip over 'dead' when finally hit with a dodgy air rifle or the fish in a plastic bag sadly lasted only a day after long efforts to spike an ace with a bent dart.

Below: This is a slightly unusual scene outside the Royal Cinema, as the queue is mostly female and there is a large can of Heinz Strained Food precariously positioned above the waiting crowd. The cinema is only a backdrop, however, as the onlookers are waiting patiently to get a view of the Queen and Royal party as they pass on their way to the opening of Bury Town Hall on 22 October, 1954. This very 'Royal' building began life as the Theatre Royal and was described as 'the most popular theatre in the north of England'. It played host to such names as Charlie Chaplin, Sir Henry Irvine and Fred Karno's Circus. Film began to take over and the ornate frontage of the Royal gave way to a more up-to-date art deco style frontage we see here. The reference to Woman's World is the 1954 film drama starring Van Heflin, Lauren Bacall and Clifton Webb, appearing on the screen at the time.

Right: Bury's Town Hall was officially opened by her Majesty the Queen Elizabeth II on the 22 October, 1954. This was some 15 years after the foundation stone was laid in 1939 by the Earl of Derby. The building was designed by Reginald Edmond as a result of an architectural competition. Work commenced on site in 1938 and, despite the war, continued until 1940, by which time only the outer shell had been completed. It remained in this incomplete state until work was able to re-commence in 1947, with only the basement being in use as an air raid shelter and the headquarters of the local Air Raid Precautions (ARP) unit.

Bury folk were delighted and honoured by the Queen's agreement to formally open the Town Hall and they turned out to welcome her in their thousands. The building was noted for its simple dignity and clean modern lines and is now the home of the Borough Council.

Below: Although opened in 1922, the Art Cinema and Café has the feel of an older era. There was a large 1st floor café utilizing the balcony void area which is now a lounge. It was sometimes advertised as the Indian Lounge Café on account of is decor! The cinema on Haymarket Street, in 1951, shows signs from the forthcoming attraction, 'The Elusive Pimpernel' and for Joan Crawford in 'Harriet Craig'. The couple entering the cinema may have be going for a bite of lunch although eating out at this time must have been for a special occasion. Films ceased in the 1960s and the building has since been utilised as a billiard hall, bingo casino, Chicago Rock Café, and since 23 October, 2009, as a pub in the J.D. Wetherspoon chain, known as the Art Picture House. The former Art Cinema is a Grade II Listed building.

Above: A few days off school, a bit of sunshine, and out come the fishing rods. Spending their spare time at Brandleholme Lodges were 14-year-olds Glynn Davenport and Lalia Mallia, seen here on an unseasonably warm day on 22 February, 1971. The camera may have captured the happy pair of chums, but whether they caught anything with their rods is not recorded. One thing we can be sure of is that at the age of 14 they were not worrying like their elders about the state of the economy, which was then rapidly going downhill, or about inflation, which within a few years would reach nearly 30 per cent. Until a week earlier beer had been just two shillings a pint. Decimalisation had arrived on 14 February, however, and the 10p pint quickly went the same way as tanners and thruppenny bits.

Left: This art-deco style building was purpose-built as a cinema in 1936. The 'Odeon' was a part of a grander scheme of super cinemas built by the Birmingham entrepreneur Oscar Deutsch. During the thirties Deutsch was opening new cinemas at a prodigious rate and in the next year would open cinemas in nearby Radcliffe and Bolton. Opening with "Twos Company" the cinema had seating for 1,500 patrons. After many successful years the cinema fell victim of the continual erosion of cinemagoers who opted to stay at home and watch the relatively recent colour TV service. The inevitable happened, and the cinema closed with the film "Mad Max" in 1981. The building lay empty until the mid-80s when it was reopened as a roller skating rink and more recently a night club.

Bury's Clarence Lido, off the A56 Walmersley Road, was completed in the summer of 1963 and started life as a reservoir. Work started in 1962 when 10,000 gallons of water were drained from the then reservoir and concrete walls replaced the boulder strewn banking. Corporation gardeners had to battle bad weather to try and get the Lido ready in time. Costing £14,000, the Lido was perhaps rightly described chairman of Bury's Recreation Grounds Committee as probably being the 'finest in the North'. It has been tailor-made for the site, and a lot of work has gone into the scheme. It could put Bury on the map as a centre for trippers. The water was probably freezing cold, but that did not stop the children in our two pictures from the late 60s enjoying themselves. The term lido is an Italian word for beach and forms part of the place name of several Italian seaside resorts. Lido seemingly found its way into English from tourists returning from the Lido di Venezia, in Venice, where sea-bathing took place from the late 19th century. The word was apparently first used for a public outdoor swimming pool in the UK in July 1935, in London.

Above: Cycling in Bury was a big deal in the 40s and 50s and still has thriving cycling groups today. It liberated people from their daily work and as cars were still out of the reach of many families in the town, cycling gave the option of seeing the countryside and even going on touring holidays. It is, however, still surprising to see a fully constructed 'banked' cycle track in the town, which was at the end of Alfred Street in front of the huge Pilot Mill. One famous Bury cyclist of this era was Reginald 'Reg' (Hargreaves) Harris, born in Birtle near Bury in 1920, who won the world amateur sprint title in 1947, two Olympic silver medals in 1948, and the professional title in 1949, 1950, 1951 and 1954. Reg surprised many of his younger admirers when he made a comeback 20 years later winning a British title in 1974 at the age of 54. Unlike the cycle track which lasted only a few years, Reg carried on into his seventies and passed away after a life of incredible cycling achievements in June 1992.

Left: A smaller ride than some in the Bury Fair, but probably even more fun for these youngsters in the 1960s who may be having their first taste of what a fairground could offer. Proud parents look on in their familiar 60s jackets and flared jeans, or are they 'loons'? The older sister holds her brother's hand patiently waiting for their turn, but which car do we want, she may be asking.

Above: Photographed here in the summer of 1973, one might be forgiven for imagining the town's library and art gallery was in some sunny Mediterranean city rather than in the usually less than sunny Lancashire. Bury Art Gallery and Museum opened in 1901 thanks to the generosity of the children of local paper manufacturer Thomas Wrigley. To commemorate Queen Victoria's Diamond Jubilee in 1897, they presented the town with their father's art collection which included paintings by Turner, Landseer and Constable, as well as a number of watercolours, engravings and Wedgwood plaques. Bury Art Gallery and Museum has a varied programme of changing exhibitions including challenging contemporary and thematic displays. The building is grade II listed. In 2005 a £1.2 million refurbishment was carried out, designed to provide a brand new museum, art gallery and library all under one roof.

Right: Though this may look like a typical example of house building in the late 1960s, first impressions can be misleading. In fact this photo from 1969 shows the Bolton Road Methodists' Sports Club pavilion under construction in June of that year. In the foreground, playing scratch cricket, are Keven Warburton aged eight, and Malcolm Bailey aged ten. More than four decades on the boys will now be middle-aged men perhaps with their own children, even grandchildren. But though the years may pass some things never change: boys were playing cricket just like this a hundred years before this scene was captured by the photographer's lens, and they are still doing so today. The only difference is that today's youngsters are more likely to own a set of factory-made stumps and bats.

Tetrosyl - A Cut Above

Tetrosyl Ltd, makers of the legendary 'T-Cut', is based in Bevis Green, Bury. The firm is the largest manufacturer and supplier of car care products in the UK. With an annual turnover of over £100 million, the privately-owned company also specialises in oils and lubricants, refinishing, and DIY products. The company has a significant worldwide presence, extending its global reach to 76 countries and is also the market leader in France.

But how did this formidable business, now a group of companies, come into being? The company's founder was a remarkable individual, Clifford Schofield.

Clifford Schofield was born on 24th January, 1923. At the time his parents, Arthur and Grace Schofield, lived at 31, Urmston Street, Oldham. A younger brother, Derek, soon followed.

Clifford was proud that his father was a monumental mason, a man with strength, patience, artistry and accuracy - skills and characteristics inherited and demonstrated by Clifford throughout his life. Clifford had great strength of character and followed both his instincts and his reasoned decisions resolutely whenever he formed a view about something to be done.

Soon after the outbreak of the Second World War, Trooper Schofield 14224981 (then aged 17) joined the Royal Artillery Corps and then later served in tank command with the 17th and 21st Lancers (and later the 16th and 5th Lancers) in Africa and

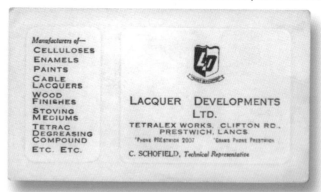

across Europe with 'the Death or Glory Boys', as the Lancers who had led the Charge of the Light Brigade were known.

Following his demobilisation at the end of the war Clifford returned to his first job, a clerical position with British Engine Insurance in Manchester.

In the evenings and at weekends he enjoyed a long-held and lucrative love of jazz, playing piano in local popular bands at dance halls all over Cheshire. It was something which he had also managed to incorporate occasionally within his army service whenever conditions permitted.

On a rare Saturday in 1950 when he wasn't playing jazz with his band, Clifford was at the Ritz dancehall in Manchester where he met Jean Bailey. They were married in 1951. Their

Top left: Founder, Clifford Schofield.
Top right: *Clifford Schofield's original business card.* ***Left:*** *A Tetrosyl truck from the early years carrying various company branding.* ***Above:*** *Tetrosyl Stopper - Filler paste of the 1950s.*

children came along in 1957, 1959 and 1961.

Meanwhile, as a junior clerical worker in a major insurance company, Clifford had stood at the foot of the career ladder, looked up and saw a long queue and a long wait in front of him in terms of career progression. Clifford's determination 'to get somewhere' overcame his natural patience and against his father's strong advice, he left the certainty of long employment and a pension with Royal Insurance and took a sales job 'cold calling', selling carbon paper and typewriter ribbons in the Cheetham Hill district of Manchester.

Becoming a salesman demonstrated Clifford's inner strength and determination. Clifford was by nature a shy person, a characteristic which stayed with him throughout his life. He also suffered from a stammer, something which he later succeeded in permanently dominating. Ambition, however, led him to leave a safe and friendly work environment for the quicker progress which he might achieve through measurable performance in a competitive sales environment. That ambition and a determination to overcome obstacles were characteristics typical of the man, and ones which were to be demonstrated time and again throughout his life. Not long into his new selling career, a chance meeting on the road with a former army colleague

opened a door for Clifford which would ultimately lead to the creation of his own business, and eventually to Tetrosyl Limited.

Clifford's former comrade in arms was working for a company called Bennett's and Hyde, the makers of 'Gunk' a degreasing product used then and now in the motor trade. There was a vacancy in the company for a sales person, Clifford explained to his pal that 'of course' he had good motor trade experience and that he was looking for a move. In fact Clifford had been successful in his job selling carbon paper, but he recognised that his opportunities to progress within the company were limited.

Clifford was offered and accepted the job selling Gunk. As part of his induction to selling his new employer's products, Clifford was introduced to the chemistry involved, a subject which he found fascinating - as he put it later: "to find that you can add one chemical to another chemical to make a product which you can sell for twice the combined price of the ingredients, was a real

Top: A bird's eye view of Bevis Green Works in the early 1960s.
Above left and below: A range of CarPlan products from the 1960s.

eye opener". That fascination with the chemistry of products and the market for such products eventually broadened Clifford's work for the company into a combined Sales and Marketing role. The exposure which this role gave to Clifford's artistic side enhanced his practical skills. Eventually however, frustration at the lack of any opportunity to join the Board at Bennett's and Hyde, led in 1954 to Clifford deciding to go it alone, and to set up as a one man band, marketing and selling his own products as Lacquer Developments Limited.

Clifford's first venture was a galvanising product, something which coincided with the early but growing popularity of television and in particular the need to weatherproof external aerials. Alongside this Clifford began to develop his motor trade market contacts, working firstly with pigments and solvents to create paint for crash repair businesses. He then broadened his product range with early examples of polyester body-fillers as a quick and effective replacement for the molten lead which had been traditionally used for that purpose.

Clifford's patience and temper were sorely tested early on in this venture when he managed to persuade a body shop foreman to look at and consider his body filler as a viable alternative to the old lead methods. Clifford had tried and tried to get an appointment to show his product to the body shop foreman. When the day finally arrived the foreman seized upon Clifford's carefully prepared finished sample of body filler, carefully shaped and painted by Clifford the previous night, and smashed it to pieces with a big hammer! For a normally quiet and shy man, Clifford had retained enough of his army vocabulary to express his views very clearly that day.

In those early days of working alone, there were inevitably setbacks. Clifford's small and limited manufacturing operation in Prestwich, within an insecure and poorly lit building, was raided more than once at night by vandals who wrecked his equipment, his stock and his materials, leaving the place in a terrible state.

*Facing page: CarPlan advertising from a motoring publication in 1966. **Top left:** CarPlan trucks were delivering throughout the UK by the mid-1960s. **Top right:** 1964 saw the launch of over 200 colours in the CarPlan Colour Service. **Centre:** Multilingual used for the first time in the 1960s. **Below:** The Tetrosyl sales force in 1966.*

Each time Clifford's determination came to the fore and he cleaned up the mess, recovered what he could and set to, regaining the ground that had been lost. Of course he was human, and of course these set backs angered and hurt him. One of these occasions briefly caused Clifford tears of disappointment and frustration, but he would not be beaten.

Despite his tears Clifford persevered. Through his dogged determination and his drive to be a success, the business developed. He was able to move from Prestwich to better premises in Radcliffe, and then in the early 1960s he moved his family to The Whitehouse at Bromley Cross, and in 1963 acquired for the business the Bevis Green site in Bury which is still today the head office of the company. Bevis Green was a former 18th century dye works, and provided an ideal base for the company's expansion plans. All did not go perfectly, however, at the new site: in August 1965 a large chemical explosion rocked the site, a blast described by

the Manchester Evening News as a 'Volcano'. Undeterred by the set back, the site was soon cleaned up and in 1969 a new purpose-built goods warehouse was completed at Bevis Green.

Meanwhile, back in its early days the company had been at first called Lacquer Developments Limited. The company's products were given the brand name of 'Tetrosyl', a unique name invented by Clifford.

Clifford soon came to realise that when he visited customers and prospective customers the name Lacquer Developments

Limited didn't mean much to them. Yet Clifford would often see on their premises, or take with him some Tetrosyl products, and these were often recognised or remembered even if the company was not.

'Lacquer Developments' just wasn't a memorable name – but Tetrosyl certainly was. The change of the company name to Tetrosyl Limited was inevitable.

Tetrosyl would become something of a family business, with Clifford's younger brother Derek, and Clifford and Jean's three children, Margot, Paul and Peter, all at one time working for the firm; although only Peter would continue to work for the company in the long term.

Probably the most famous Tetrosyl product is T-Cut, a name which like Hoover has progressed

Top left: The aftermath of the large chemical explosion in 1965. *Top right:* A new purpose-built goods warehouse at Bevis Green was completed in 1969. *Centre:* CarPlan Triplewax and Tetrion all-purpose filler television advertisements in the early 1970s. *Left:* Peter Schofield in 1977, around the time he joined the firm full-time. *Below:* The expanded Triplewax brand of products in the 1980s.

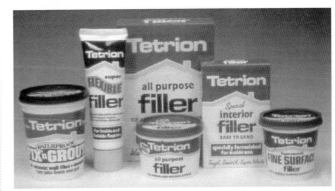

from a noun to a verb in the English language, "I am going to T-Cut my car before I sell it" is a common phrase amongst motorists.

The product T-Cut was invented by Clifford to fill a gap in the market which he had spotted. In the old days, body shops would use Brasso to blend or 'feather-in' the edges of re-sprayed paintwork to match the existing body work.

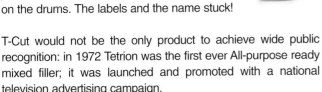

Clifford realised that Brasso was fairly harsh for such use, and so in 1958 he set about producing a gentler, paint-friendly version. T-Cut became an industry best seller, and it still is.

In the early days, when he was filling some drums with his new product, Clifford didn't have a name or any labels for it. Having built the company up from nothing, Clifford was careful with his money and so, prudently took some surplus Tetrosyl Cutting Oil labels and cut and joined the words to make 'T-Cut' and glued these on the drums. The labels and the name stuck!

T-Cut would not be the only product to achieve wide public recognition: in 1972 Tetrion was the first ever All-purpose ready mixed filler; it was launched and promoted with a national television advertising campaign.

Despite the successes enjoyed by the business as it grew, there were of course setbacks, some unsuccessful business ventures and losses of investments. Under Clifford's leadership, however, the company was always ready to re-adjust its focus, to learn from mistakes, and above all to do what it still does best: manufacturing, marketing and selling to specific markets which it knows and understands.

Clifford's health had its ups and downs, he had a triple heart by-pass in 1991, and shingles for a period of three years and septicaemia later in the 1990s. Yet, he was never away from the office for a day longer than absolutely necessary. He returned to the office full time only three weeks after his heart by-pass and worked every day throughout the shingles period; work was simply his life: Clifford retired in August 2005, handing the reins to his son Peter.

Top left: An aerial view of Bridge Hall in the mid-1980s. **Centre:** *Various Tetrosyl products: CarPlan Colour Service with a unique tamper evident cap, relaunched in the early 1980s; Carlube Oils, launched in 1988, and Tetrosyl All Seasons 5* Anti-freeze which was invented and patented in 1992.* **Bottom:** *A Tetrosyl chemist colour matching (left), in house design studio (centre) and the research and development centre (right) in the 1990s.* **Top right:** *A range of Tetrion products relaunched in the late 1990s.*

'The Chairman', as Clifford Schofield will long be remembered at Tetrosyl, passed away in 2007 – an unusual and gifted man, noted for his ability, determination and a quiet sense of humour.

Today Peter Schofield is Chairman of Tetrosyl. Under his leadership the company founded by his father offers a 'one stop shop' to customers, providing complete product ranges supported by visionary marketing, category management, product and packaging development, patented technology and distribution efficiency. A culture of continuous improvement and entrepreneurship ensures that Tetrosyl can adapt quickly to the changing needs of a complex and competitive market.

Staff at Tetrosyl are united through passion and pride in its market leading brands. These include Carlube, Tetrion, Aqua-T, Autopratic, and, of course, CarPlan, which boasts the instantly recognisable names of both T-Cut and Triplewax. Tetrosyl's dedicated marketing strategy is implemented through design effectiveness, consistent product quality, and total availability. Brand awareness

is reinforced through high profile sponsorship and effective advertising.

The Tetrosyl Group now also encompasses Maccess, the largest distributor of car care and accessories in the UK with 14 branches and over 25,000 product lines. Motor World, founded as Bradford Motor Spares in 1968, is the largest independent car parts and accessories retailer with over 100 stores in England and Wales. Tetrosyl International was established in 1975 – and now trades in 76 countries as Europe's leading producer of branded and private label automotive products. Tetrosyl France, based near Lille, is the leading supplier of car care products in France. Tetrosyl I-Tec is the intellectual property arm of the Group, which owns and manages brands, patents and formulations - today these also include the Wonder Wheels and Bluecol brand trade marks. FCA Ltd manages the Group's freehold properties – not least its £10 million distribution centre at Chadderton.

Now, more than half a century since this award-winning business was founded by Clifford Schofield, Tetrosyl really can boast of being 'a cut above the rest'.

Facing page: CarPlan T-cut advertising from the 1960s. **Top pictures:** Tetrosyl's Bevis Green Works (top left), Greengate Distribution Centre (inset to top left) and large storage tank capacity at the Bridge Hall site (top right). **Centre page:** Clifford Schofield pictured during retirement. **Above:** Group Chairman, Peter Schofield. **Left and above left:** The new livery of Carlube trucks introduced in 2011 and revolutionary new self drying car shampoo launched in January 2011.

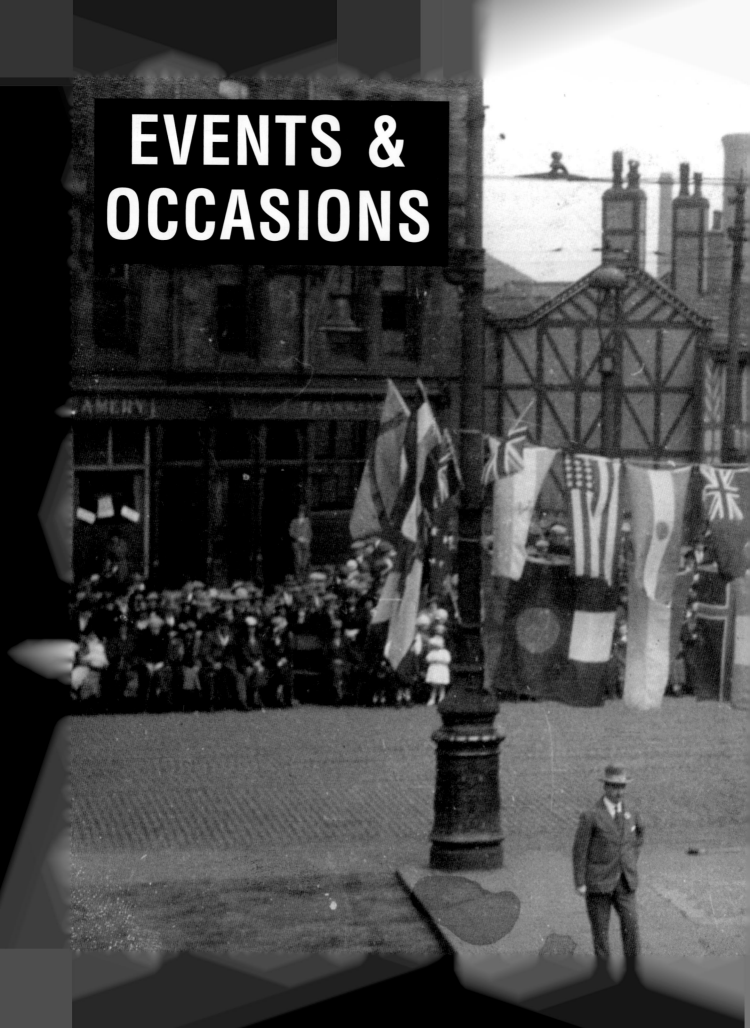

EVENTS & OCCASIONS

It's Whit Friday in the Market Place Bury in 1924. The bunting is out for what promises to be a bumper day of festivities. These days Whitsuntide seems to have got rather lost on our calendars, having been replaced in 1967 by the secular Spring Bank Holiday. Back in the days when every child attended Sunday School, however, we knew all about Whitsuntide, or Pentecost to give it its rather more formal name. Whitsunday is the seventh Sunday after Easter, which commemorates the descent of the Holy Spirit upon Christ's disciples, according to the Acts of the Apostles. Few however would know that Whitsunday or 'White Sunday' derived its name from the white garments worn by 'catechumens', those expecting to be baptised on that Sunday, when infant baptism was still uncommon. Throughout the north west huge church and chapel parades called Whit Walks took place. Typically, the parades contained brass bands and choirs; girls attending often dressed in white. Whit Fairs too were commonplace.

Top left: Everyone looks cheerful in the photo – even the ox which doesn't yet know that it is shortly to be the centre of a good deal of enjoyment. The occasion in June 1911 is an ox-roast in Bury to celebrate an important national event. Queen Victoria's son King Edward VII had died on 6 May, 1910, at Buckingham Palace. He was succeeded by his eldest son George V, who was proclaimed King around the country in the following week. King George's coronation took place on 22 June, 1911, and was marked by celebrations across the whole of Britain and the world, so much of which was then coloured pink on the map. King George, like his father before him, was not just a king, but also the Emperor of India.

Left: It's 1919 and this military monster isn't quite what it seems. This is only a mock-up not the real thing. This civic occasion is clearly an event connected to the end of the Great War in 1918. Though the picture has no caption the most likely explanation is that the photograph was taken prior to the first Armistice Day church service at 11 o'clock on 11 November, 1919. The tank was very much a symbol of victory over the Germans and their allies. Years of squalid and stalemate trench warfare had only ended when the British had invented the tank, a machine capable of crossing trenches and running through barbed-wire entanglements, allowing our lads to at last get at the enemy without being mown down by machine-gun fire.

Above: Under the Bury Improvement Act 1846 a board of 27 improvement commissioners was formed for Bury. The Improvement Commissioners District was enlarged in 1872. A charter of incorporation dated 9 September, 1876, made the town a municipal borough. Fifty years later, in September 1926, the town celebrated its Golden Jubilee with parades and numerous other civic events. Part of the parade is pictured here: with no intentional irony one young person in the parade is the personification of trade. Yet within a very short time it would be the lack of trade which would send Bury, Britain and the rest of world into a cycle of economic depression which would last throughout the 1930s, and which tragically only the massive cost and expenditure of a world war would cure.

Above: The day dawned damp and murky, but no-one on Norman Street, now itself part of history, seemed to have a care in the world. This was the day that Queen Elizabeth II was being crowned in Westminster Abbey and 2 June, 1953 was going to become a part of folklore. Bunting bedecked the street and Union flags hung from windows and telegraph poles. We might have lived in humble surroundings, but we knew how to party and there were festivities the like of which we had not seen since VJ Day in 1945. Down in London crowds turned out in the rain and watched the coronation procession of foreign royals and dignitaries go past. One of the most endearing memories is of a beaming Salote, Queen of Tonga, waving to everyone from an open topped carriage that was gradually filling with rain. On Norman Street, the residents tucked into butties and buns and the children played street games of musical chairs on ones dragged out from kitchens. An old wind-up gramophone played 'She wears red feathers' by Guy Mitchell and all the little ones joined in with Lita Roza's 'How much is that doggie in the window?' Rumour had it that someone round the corner had a television set and was watching the ceremony being described by Richard Dimbleby. Now, there was posh.

Right and facing page Tom Ryan, aged 50, and Clifford Savage, aged 15, are being interviewed here after they survived the collapse of a three-storey building in Haymarket Street on 25 November, 1955. Debris had been scattered all over the road. Back in those days a cup of tea and a Woodbine would cure anything – no need for counselling for post traumatic shock syndrome, never mind time off work to recover.

Left and below: Utter devastation was the scene the day after a major blaze destroyed the market hall in November 1968. Visitors looked on in disbelief at the twisted remains of the once-proud building. This elevated view, framed by the early morning November mist shows the full extent of the damage; it must have been obvious to 'those in the know' that the idea of rebuilding the facility was a non-starter. There was sadness too for the scores of traders who had lost there means of earning a living in the blaze. No doubt some of them will be featured in this photograph, looking at the scene of devastation and wondering what the future was to hold for them. The photograph below graphically highlights just how extensive the damage was. At street level the casual observer may have been forgiven for thinking that the fire had caused serious, but superficial damage, after all, the distinctive domed roof of the market hall and the shop fronts of the businesses which surrounded it all

respected, post-war politicians, Barbara Castle – Baroness Castle of Blackburn as she later became. At the time this picture was taken Mrs Castle had left Westminster to become Euro MP for Manchester North. Elected to Parliament in 1945 as Labour MP for Blackburn, she rose to become one of the most important Labour Party politicians of the twentieth century. In the Wilson governments of 1964–1970 and 1974-76, she held a succession of ministerial posts. As Minister of Transport, she introduced the breathalyser to combat drink-driving, and also made permanent the 70mph speed limit. One of her most memorable achievements as Transport minister was to pass legislation decreeing that all new cars had to be fitted with seat-belts. She died in 2002.

Below: Labour MP John Prescott was in Bury in 1988 to officially open the Economic Development Unit. John Leslie Prescott was born on 31 May, 1938 in Prestatyn, North Wales. Known in the media as 'Two Jags' Prescott because of his liking for Jaguar cars. He was a colourful character in a Parliament often filled with far duller figures. Always a popular figure with the public because of his working class origins and his blunt honesty.

seemed to be generally intact. This slightly elevated view shows that the fire had destroyed virtually everything apart from these features, and that the idea of repairing the market could not even be considered.

Above: 'Adult Education 1983-84. What Do You want?' asks the 'Live and Learn' newsletter. Holding the paper is one of Britain's most well-known, and well-

regular, militia and volunteers who died in South Africa between 1900 and 1902. The memorial has metal inscribed plaques, one on each of the four sides. The names of the fallen are listed in alphabetical order within rank. The memorial was unveiled on 18 March, 1905, by the 17th Earl of Derby; the sculptor was Sir George James Frampton.

Above: Bury's Boer War memorial is to be found in Whitehead Gardens, known as Clock Tower Gardens, in front of the Town Hall. Originally situated in Market Place, the memorial was being moved in the 1980s when threatened by the traffic. The memorial is a bronze statue of a soldier standing in Fusilier's dress, waving his cap. The plinth on which it stands has an inscription which lists the 170 men from the Lancashire Fusiliers,

Below: It can be windy at times in Bury. Indeed it can be a bit breezy anywhere at any time all over Lancashire. Usually little damage is done but occasionally the effects are dramatic. Here, for example, is the effect of 'a bit of a breeze' in Bolton Road where a tree has been blown down, completely blocking the carriageway. Storm force winds are nothing novel in Bury, but in October 1987 BBC weatherman Michael Fish made the boob of his career when he announced after the six o'clock news that rumours of a hurricane heading for Britain were nothing to worry about – it wasn't going to happen. The next morning the weatherman had to eat his words: all across Britain thousands of trees were down, and many buildings damaged.

Above: In Britain today all policemen are commonly referred to as 'Bobbies'. Originally though, they were also known as 'Peelers' in reference to our own, Sir Robert Peel. To be a 'Peeler' the rules were quite strict; you had to be male, 6ft tall and have no history of any wrong-doings. Today, the criteria is directed less towards height and sex and more towards physical fitness and being of good character. The Peelers, became the model for the creation of all the provincial forces, after the passing of the County Police Act in 1839. Ironically however, Bury was the only major town which elected not to have its own separate police force. The town remained part of the Lancashire Constabulary until 1974. In this picture above, it's nice to see these smart and traditional looking bobbies parading at the Peel Monument outside Bury parish church, wearing proper uniforms and helmets.

Right: Taken in 1983, people can be seen outside Peel Tower on Holcombe Hill. The 128 ft tall tower is in memory of one of Bury's most famous residents, Sir Robert Peel, former Prime Minister of the United Kingdom and founder of the Metropolitan Police Service. A public subscription provided the £1,000 needed to build the tower. The stone was obtained from the hillside, high above Ramsbottom and the Tower was opened in September 1852. It had been built in such haste that the necessary permission had not been obtained from the landowner the land, the Duke of Buccleuch. This matter was only rectified in 1868 when the land was transferred into the keeping of six trustees. The tower closed in 1947 and was reopened and rededicated in November 1985 by Councillor Alice Maders.

AT THE SHOPS

Right: Miss M.A. Cooper's tea rooms in Bury present a tempting sight. The window display is especially interesting, with not only the obvious cake stands and cakes as one might expect but also featuring an attractively dressed doll. The tea rooms are pictured here in the early 1900s. Tea rooms were an important part of the social history of the period and respectable places where nice folk could meet socially. This was in stark contrast to pubs. The temperance movement was in full swing, and tea rooms flourished on the back of it. Joseph Livesey started his Temperance Movement in Preston in 1832, requiring followers to sign a pledge of total abstinence. The Band of Hope was founded in Leeds

in 1847, with the aim of saving working class children from the perils of drink. Nonconformists were especially active, with large numbers of Baptists, Methodists and Congregationalists being teetotal.

Bottom left: What a truly phenomenal display this is at O'Rourke's Fruit and Vegetable Stall in Bury market. What an enormous amount of effort must have gone in to putting it all together – and what memories it evokes. Yet according to scientists it's not your sense of vision applied to a picture that is most likely to bring back lost memories, nor sounds or touch, but smell. Try it yourself: get a potato, a cabbage and an orange then shut your eyes and smell them. Does it instantly take you back to childhood, holding mother's hand as she shops for food in the market? Now do you recall

hopefully tugging at mother's coat to suggest that perhaps she had spent too much time chatting and you were getting cold and hungry?

Below: When food was sourced, bought and cooked by the seasons, it provided a naturally varied diet for the people of Bury, not quite the same today where consumer demand has required that almost all foods are available all year round. E Derby was providing its 'Lamb Season' offerings in this 1926 photo of one of the many shops which surrounded the market hall. Their delivery boy looks smart in his apron, shirt and tie and no doubt the highlight of his day was to cycle around the town delivering the likes of lamb and bunches of mint to the many customers of E Derby's, Quality Butchers, Bury, Telephone number 410!

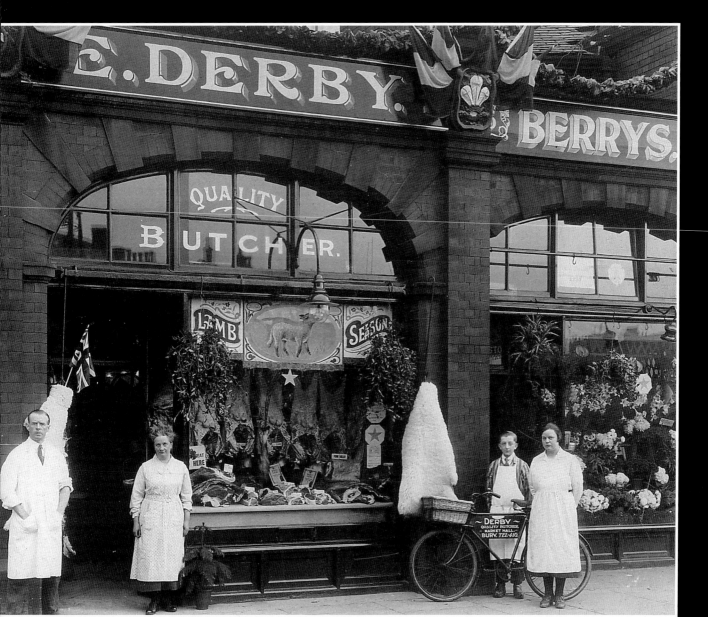

There has surely never been a finer building in Bury than the Market Hall. And what better exemplifies its solid down to earth attitude that John Cox whose premises can be seen on the left: John Cox advertises himself not as a tripe dresser , but as a dresser of high class tripe. Only in Bury! Ainsworth's wholesale confectioners is to the right of Cox's premises and features a classic Fry's Chocolates advert. On the far right are the premises of H Halstead and A Derby. Built in 1901 with 60 stalls, the Bury Market Hall was the jewel in the crown of Bury markets which for centuries has made the town a magnet for folk from all over Lancashire. Bury Market Hall has rightly been described as one of the best equipped and most architecturally striking market halls in the North West.

Halstead's 'Provision Merchants' in old market is pictured here in 1936. It's a good illustration of how things used to be: no modern day nonsense about refrigeration for the bacon swinging from hooks above the staff. Flies wouldn't do any harm - the hams were smoked well enough in those days to keep anything nasty at bay. One of the main products on show seems to be 'Lively Polly'. This was actually a dry soap, which apparently would wash clothes without rubbing. Quite revolutionary for the time and enabled the woman of the house to do 'A day's work before dinnertime'. On the right is a fixture of this period, and indeed of the whole of history until the 1940s - the shop boy. In the early 20th century the school leaving age was just 12 but was raised to 15 in 1944. Before the war most folk left school at 14, and adverts for a 'willing lad' to work in a shop were commonplace.

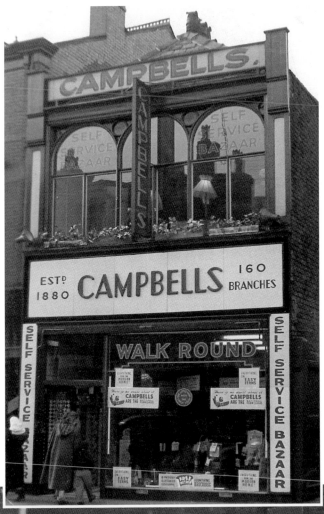

Left: Campbells Self Service Bazaar was established in 1880 and might have been one of a family of stores in Bury. Other Campbells shops in the town included a grocers and a furniture store, but we can only assume the connection. There is a link, however, which may have been a sign of the times in 1935, as the Bazaar has four window signs offering 'Easy Terms' and the store suggested you could furnish your home for £1 per month. That was not the only boast made by Campbells, as they also claim in their window advertising that with 160 branches, 'There is no doubt about it Campbells are the National Furnishers'. Quite a statement, even in those days!

Bottom: Heinz Spaghetti was a relatively new tinned food in 1951 as the company extended their '57 Varieties' advertising as they did on the corner of Butcher Lane. St Bruno Tobacco, Will's Capstan Navy Cut, Star, Gold Flake and Robin cigarettes are the other prominent advertisements drawing people into this newsagents near The Rock. No chance of these types of adverts appearing today given the many health problems associated with the smoking.

Did you know?

The name Bury, also earlier known as 'Buri' and 'Byri', comes from an Old English word meaning castle stronghold or fort - an early form of modern English borough.

Above: Timothy Whites & Taylors Chemist shop was on the corner of the attractive Hornby Buildings built by the corporation in 1933. Many readers will remember this chemists chain as they would have visited for their cough and cold remedies and prescriptions. It looks like H Stones Butchers has closed for the day as the front window blind is pulled fully down. The Hornby Buildings were well liked in the town and were lit up for two weeks after the initial opening and again in 1936 for the Jubilee of King George.

Left: The Rock, 1950, from the Maypole dairy on the left and down almost its full length. The centrally placed street lights, suspended on wires from standards on the pavement, add a touch of 'olde worlde' to the photograph. Lamps held within concrete posts were still a few years away. When this scene was captured we were at the exact halfway point of the century. In 1900 the 20th century dawned with a monarch coming to the end of her reign. War was raging in South Africa, trade unions formed the beginnings of the Labour Party and an international exhibition was held in Paris. In 1950 our monarch was in his last years, a war began in Korea, the Labour Party was in government and preparations were made for the Festival of Britain to be held the following year. There were some similarities, it seems, with life in late Victorian times, but the differences were far more numerous. In 1900 there were no aeroplanes, radio, television, widespread use of electricity, penicillin, X-rays or atomic fission. We had come a long way, though there was still much to do, especially in putting the 'Great' back into Britain as we tried to undo the economic harm of two world wars.

Above: Another store of Timothy White's the Chemist is on the corner where people are hurrying across The Rock in July 1963. Whites was a popular chain which was providing its pharmacy service to the people of Bury until it was taken over by Boots in 1968. Just behind the double decker bus we can see Fred Dawes' television rental shop. A real boost to the television trade came in June 1953 with the Queen's coronation which everyone wanted to see, but only a few would have the means to rent a small black and white set for the corner of their room. That said, neighbours were always welcome to pop in during the 50s and 60s and many certainly did if you had a telly. A few programmes stood the test of time such as 'Steptoe and Son' and 'No Hiding Place', not quite the full colour HD, BBC iPlayer on-demand world we know these days, but great entertainment all the same.

to the market specially to buy one of Thompson's black puddings, piping hot in a grease-proof paper. There was a special buzz around the market and something for everyone with stall providing fresh produce and famous characters, like 'Cheap Jack'. Many will remember his patter as he gathered crowds of people around his stall to flog them his household goods at 'knockdown prices!!'

Above: An elevated view of Bury which seems to be all roofs, but look closely and you can see the covered market in the centre and the spire of Bury Parish Church in the distance. The Queens Hotel is in the darker buildings on the right of the picture. Bury has a reputation as one of the busiest and best markets in the north west. Shoppers travel from miles around and travel in by the coach load to sample the delights of Bury Market stalls. Many older readers will fondly remember going

Below: Shoppers were oblivious to the high level photographer taking snaps of them on this sunny day at Bury Market in 1968. Ladies with prams, old gents with their flat caps, regardless of the heat and children dragging mum to Granelli's ice cream van in the foreground, for a cornet, with 'raspberry drips' of course, to cool them down. No doubt a few would be working out the new decimal coin system introduced that year so that they did not get 'diddled' out of their change.

Above: "Get your turkeys, geese capons and fresh ducklings here, best prices in town"! was a regular call from the Quality Stall in Bury market as the young chap sold his produce of fish and game. The lady with the 'bobbed' hair style seems to be interested in a packed chicken and the lady at the boxes with a coat with leopard skin collar is searching for her purse, not sure if the price can be brought lower than the tags suggest. Market days were all-important to Bury traders and shoppers. They provided a sense of certainty, fresh food would be available, and the stall holders were confident that shoppers would be there and willing to buy – if the price was right.

Right: The Moss Street side of the market shows the stalls with their string of light bulbs to lighten the gloom and show their produce at its best, The smells and aromas from these stalls stays in the memory forever and this 1960s photo shows how busy the market was. Not just on a Saturday, as it was until 1947, but then Wednesdays and after 1953

Friday was also added as a market day. What loyalty of both shoppers and traders, and all without store cards and bonus points!

TRANSPORT

Right: A very early photograph indeed; this scene captures the forerunner of the Bury to Whitefield bus service – the Bury to Whitefield horse-drawn omnibus. Public transport began some time in the early 19th century and in 1817 there were coach services being run between Manchester and Bury along Bury Old Road, which had been constructed in 1755. The Coach and Horses public house at Kirkhams was the coaching inn. Bury New Road – a turnpike road, taking an alternative route - was constructed in 1827. Toll bars were built at Kersal Bar, Besses o' th' Barn, Stand Lane and Blackford Bridge. In the 1860s and 1870s transport consisted of a four-horse bus running at hourly intervals from Whitefield, with local passenger stops at the Bay Horse Inn at Chapelfield and at the Church Inn.

Below: Wilson & Stockall was owned by Cliff Holden Motors from 1963 to 1966. The workshops were on Rochdale Road in Bury adjacent to the new Angouleme Way roundabout. In 1902 the company exhibited at the Crystal Palace in London and won Gold, Silver and Bronze awards for auxilliary ambulances, yeomanry carriages and police prisoner transportation vehicles. These were all horse-drawn. It was not until later that mechanically propelled vehicles were assembled up to about the mid-1950s when the design of ambulances changed from wood and alloy carriages to full aluminium pressed panels.

Right: Thomas Suthers of the Nell Carr bakery in Shuttleworth is posing here with the latest wonder of the age – the motorised delivery van. The photographer captured this fine vehicle and its owner in Bury sometime before the First World War, but otherwise almost nothing is now known about Mr Suthers or his bakery. Perhaps you can fill in the gap. The van would appear to be a very early Ford, notably travelling on solid rubber tyres rather than on pneumatic tyres which would soon become the norm. Horseless carriages were based on horse-drawn carriages, and it took quite some time for manufactures to realise that the driver didn't need to be exposed

t's ten to four one afternoon in the 1920s. All's well with the world and the Lancashire and Yorkshire Railway is running the trains on time from Bury's Bolton Street Station to every part of Britain. Trams may get you round the town, but a fast trip to Manchester, or even far away London, means getting aboard a train pulled by a real steam locomotive, the most powerful and fastest thing on land. No wonder small boys wanted to be engine drivers when they grew up. The train's nemesis, the motor car, had already arrived on the scene, but it would be many decades before cars became fast enough and roads good enough to make then top dog in the transport stakes.

Left: London may have a more famous Fleet Street than Bury, but surely not even London can boast a finer street scene captured for posterity in the early decades of the twentieth century. The open-topped tram trundling away from us is just passing Jacksons Stores, and next to it Liptons. Criss-crossing the street are the electric cables for the tramcars which draw their power down from the long arms protruding from the top of the vehicles – always a tricky arrangement for top deck passengers when trams passed under low bridges and the cable came dangerously down near to head height. Electrification of towns and street lighting frequently followed the introduction of trams – their power cable forming the first electricity distribution grid.

Below: Saturday afternoon at the football and the tram to Gigg Lane would get you there. It was the 1930s and football was very much the national game and for Bury it was no exception. The Shakers had won the FA Cup twice already and still held the winning score and margin in their final against Derby with a 6-0 trouncing. Flat caps and trilbys were the headwear for the chaps but we can see only one lady in the queue for the tram, as the policemen and conductors watch the orderly boarding.

Above: The electric tram in the foreground rattling over the steel rails set in granite setts was one of a group that had served Bury since 1903. In this 1930s photo we see the electric trams alongside the 'new fangled' motor bus, its modern rival. The ornate tram standards carried the electric cables which provided the trams' energy, and which no doubt intrigued the young lad in short trousers just crossing the road. This was all overseen by the memorial to John Kay in Kay Gardens behind.

Right: A fine example of a sturdy petrol-driven open-back truck which was used by Gardner's solid fuel wholesale and retail distributors in Bury around the late 1940s. Gardners used to move around 3,000 tons of coal a week which required them to relocate from Oram Street to two other sites, one at Buckley Wells in Bury, and the other at Heywood Railway Station. As we know, domestic use of coal reduced in favour of the cleaner electricity and gas options, but industry and the public sector became the focus for Gardners and this required much heavier vehicles.

Top right: Cycling proficiency tests were an important part of any teenagers progress to adulthood. This young lad seems to be struggling a little with a bike slightly too big for him but he

looks determined to succeed, in his crumpled socks and black pumps. This scene is at the junction of Spring Lane and Blackburn Street in 1950. The Proficiency Officer is checking the lad's competency as part of the test and will ask further questions about the Highway Code and cycle maintenance. Hopefully, the young chap has been listening in his weekly cycle lessons and doing his homework. The Cenotaph in the background was unveiled in November 1922 to remember those who gave their lives in the Great War. Sadly, it had to be updated after WW II to commemorate those other brave Bury soldiers who also lost their lives.

Retailers at Bury's new £350m shopping centre, The Rock, opened their doors for the first time in 2010. The scheme by developer, Hammerson, transformed the town centre, creating three new department stores, 60 shops, a cinema, bowling alley and 400 flats. Anchored by Marks & Spencer and Debenhams, the development is estimated to have created 500 new jobs. How times change: here is a picture of a different time, and what might almost be a different planet. What happened to Martin's Bank? We know only too well what happened to Woolworths. Stead & Simpson is still a well known name but what about Downhan Mill Furnishing Ironmongers, and Van Allen? It's only half a century ago or so since this photograph was taken, well within living memory, but how things have changed.

Above: Knowsley Street in 1964 presents an extraordinarily quiet scene. A few folk are ambling across the zebra crossing though they haven't got much traffic to worry about. In fact, you'd be hard pressed to spot a moving car on the road. For many the years 1963-64 marked the turning point between historic and modern times. Before then the world was still drab and dreary, only slowly recovering from rationing, the war years, and before that the great Depression. Not until the early 1960s did colour return to lives long blighted by worry over how to earn a living and sometimes how to stay alive at all. The Swinging Sixties, however, drew a line under the past. The Beatles, mini-skirts, Tops of the Pops and new Prime Minister Harold Wilson's promise of the 'White-hot heat of technology' energised and enthused Britons.

Right: What a opportunity for car spotters this 1966 picture makes. Traffic has stopped for a few moments at the lights outside the Westminster Bank. Leading the pack as if they are on the starting grid for the Grand Prix are a Ford Anglia and an Austin 1100. Taking centre stage, however, is a Morris Oxford V series. Some 87,000 of these prestige vehicles were produced between 1959 and 1961. The very similar VI series sold 200,000 before production ceased in 1971. By contrast the Ford Anglia 105E, introduced in 1959, sold over a million. The Austin 1100, introduced in 1962, also passed the million mark – if one also counts the 1300 variant. Few cars from the 1960s survive to the present day – rust proofing was in its infancy.

Left: Knowsley Sreet Station was one of two Bury stations and was built by the Manchester and Leeds Railway Company in 1848. The service operated between Bury and Liverpool and transported many families to the coastal resorts in the summer months. Sadly, the last passenger left this station in October 1970 before it was demolished in 1971.

Above: Scammell introduced its three-wheeled 'Mechanical Horse' in the UK in 1934. From the late 1920s railway companies had been searching for a vehicle that would replace the horse drawn carriage. The London and North Eastern Railway's project was sold to Scammell Lorries, where the original Mechanical Horse was designed by O.D North. One of its unique features was that it automatically coupled and uncoupled with trailers. It remained largely unchanged until the late 1940s when the tractor section was redesigned creating the Scammell Scarab. This featured the same successful automatic coupling from the original but now used the Scammell 2,090cc side valve engine. Production of the Scarab ceased in 1967 and was replaced with the Scammell Townsman that now featured a fibreglass cab. Despite numerous improvements, the Townsman was mainly only sold to British Rail and the Royal Mail and production ended in 1968.

Right: The Bolton Street railway station was opened by the East Lancashire Railway in 1846 as Bury station. The ELR was absorbed by the Lancashire & Yorkshire Railway in 1859. The station was renamed Bury Bolton Street in 1866 and rebuilt in the 1880s. The street frontage burnt down after the Second World War and was replaced with a new brick and concrete entrance and footbridge in 1954. BR closed the station in 1980, the year of this photograph, when it was replaced by a new Bury station, now the terminus of the light rail link from Manchester. Since re-opening as part of the heritage railway operated by the East Lancashire Railway, a new platform building, incorporating a facade from the former Bury tram depot, has been erected on the up platform, with further refurbishment and redevelopment underway.

Above: This picture illustrates the transition at Gardners solid fuel merchants to much heavier distribution options and shows their rolling stock on the East Lancs Railway on the Bury to Rawtenstall line.

A WORKING LIFE

Above: Bedlam Green, part of The Rock triangle, was part of medieval Bury. There is little left of the ancient town, and not much left of the later town built over it. One such building was the factory of John Slater who manufactured soda water here a century ago. Had Mr Slater been a better businessman then, the world might today be drinking Bury-cola or riding on the Slater-Max at Blackpool. England's Joseph Priestley invented soda water when he first forced carbon dioxide into water in the 1770s. But it was not until 1831, when German-Swiss Johann Jacob Schweppe was awarded 'By Appointment' status by William IV, that the first 'pop' fortune was made. Thousands of businessmen attempted to emulate Schweppe's success, only a very few have succeeded.

Did you know?

The original coat of arms was granted in 1877. The symbols represented local industry and the motto was "Vincit Omnia Industria" meaning "work conquers all"

Left: Beer was stronger in the olden days. At least that's what old folk used to say. And it was true. The Defence of the Realm Act of 1914 amongst its other provisions reduced the strength of beer. That may have made an increase in workload for these two dray men pictured here n 1913 as folk needed to drink more beer to get as drunk as they were accustomed to. Maybe the draymen drank more too. It was thirsty work being a drayman delivering barrels of beer to pubs, even if the horses did most of the hard work. Draymen often got a free pint at each pub they delivered to. Not a problem when the horses knew their own way back to the brewery, but a major problem once horses were swapped for lorries.

Below: The Wellington Barracks and the adjacent Wellington Hotel look rather quiet in this early photograph. Even the horse outside the pub looks as though it has given up for the day. Outside London, many new barracks were built during the period of the anti-Corn Law riots in the 1840s, the Reform Bill riots of the 1830s and Chartist agitation 1838 to 1848. In the first half of the 19th Century rapid industrialisation was causing social and political stress. Falling real wages, unemployment and bad harvests were exacerbated by local conditions. Particularly hard hit groups were those communities whose skills and livelihoods were rendered obsolete by mechanisation in the textile industry, such as East Lancashire. The barracks at Bury were built between 1842 and 1845, for two companies of infantry - 270 men and a 48 man troop of horse.

Bottom: In today's sanitised, shrink-wrapped world of supermarket meat counters it is hard to grasp what our forbears once regularly experienced. Before the Victorian enthusiasm for cleaning up our towns and cities the business of translating meat on the hoof to meat on the table was incredibly messy and smelly. Streets where butchers plied their trade were quite literally 'a shambles' and the word 'carnage' meant exactly what today it only implies. Roads were frequently filled with animals being driven to slaughter, the sound of their bleating and bellowing an everyday experience. Streets literally ran with blood. The smell was indescribable. Something had to be done. Bury like most towns needed a proper, hygienic abattoir where order rather than chaos would prevail. And surely no northern town did better than Bury.

Right: These five Edwardian abattoir workers from Bury must have been photographed before the start of their shift rather than afterwards. Working in the abattoir was an onerous business indeed, and not a job for the faint-hearted. Slaughter was not the mechanised and instant process it would be a hundred years later. Poleaxes rather than electric stun guns were still the order of the day. White aprons and overalls might be put on in the morning, but after an hour or two on the job few abattoir employees would manage to look as clean and tidy as these five fine fellows. After an eight hour shift those employed in slaughtering and subsequent butchering would often as not be covered in gore from head to foot.

Left: Just a door and a window with a small sign outside, but this tiny cottage in Union Street, Bury, pictured in 1965 is world famous, for it was from here at Casewell's that black puddings were sent all over the globe. Today the Bury Black Pudding Company is the only manufacturer of Bury Black Pudding actually based in the town. You can find them on Bury Market. The market stall is one of the longest-standing stalls on Bury's famous market and has been trading for half a century, where generations of families continue to come and buy the firm's famous black puddings, fresh farm eggs, chickens, cheese and sausage. You'll find them at Stall No 5, Edward Block, Bury Open Market.

Below: Black pudding first came to the UK through European monks in the form of 'bloodwurst' but was later adapted with secret recipies and found a home in the town of Bury. The Black pudding stall in Bury became famous and celebrities with a taste for this northern delicacy would often drop in to taste the real thing direct from the centre of the black pudding world. Is this Geoffrey Howe about to taste the best Bury's stall could offer to visiting dignitaries? He certainly looks keen to have a try.

Above: 'Aye up Mr Herriot!' Well, not quite. James Herriot's famous stories of his life as a country vet not only took place in Yorkshire rather than Lancashire, but they had yet to be written when this picture was taken in Bury. The Richmond Veterinary Surgery was clearly what would today be called a 'mixed practice' since not only has a horse been taken in for treatment but also a collection of various dogs. Before the advent of the motor car, and indeed for long afterwards, the horse was the main means of transport. Vets or at least 'horse doctors' were as common then as garages are today. A 'veterinary surgeon' was a cut above the 'horse doctor' and his bills would reflect his greater professional expertise. The word 'Veterinarian' was first used in print by Thomas Browne in 1646 and at first meant little more than someone who worked with animals. The profession was not regulated until well into the 20th century.

Bottom left: Crikey! A two-seater tricycle, whatever next? What a monster of a machine. This vehicle was a rarity even in 1895 when it and one of its riders was captured for posterity by a cameraman eager to preserve the image for future generations. Delivering soap was clearly hard work if it needed two men to do the pedalling. Indeed it doesn't take much imagination to work out just how heavy a full load must have been in that huge box. But maybe two men were cheaper to employ than a horse. Sunlight soap was produced by Lever Brothers in 1884. Sunlight was the world's first packaged, branded laundry soap. Intended for washing clothes and general household use, the success of the product led to the name for the company's village for its workers: Port Sunlight. The formula for the soap was invented by a Bolton chemist named William Hough Watson, who was also an early business partner.

Below: How the world has changed. And what an extraordinarily vivid picture the photographer has captured of Balderstone around the time of Queen Victoria's death. The details tell of a world on the edge of modern times: a telegraph pole festooned with wires hints at the instant communication now possible thanks to electricity. The street light on the right reminds us that night time darkness has been banished. Yet there is still much of an eternal past to be seen: a horse and trap, and cattle being driven down the road which is as yet to benefit from either cobbles or tarmac. Women in the distance are wearing clogs and shawls – normal day wear, not the Sunday best reserved for church and the photographers' studio poses.

Above: Locomotive number 42644 leaving Bury Bolton Street Station on its way to Bacup. On board was the Three Counties Tour which had been organised for the Manchester Rail Travel Society. The picture was taken at 11.09 on Saturday 26 November, 1966. Quite apart from the train featured here, the photograph is an interesting record of a well-known local landmark, Bury Power Station. It may seem strange to younger people that a power station should be located so close to the centre of town, particularly as these facilities produced much pollution. This, however, was entirely typical of northern towns.

Right: Here's Blackford Brow, Manchester Road, a century ago. No prizes for guessing what's going on: the workmen are laying tracks for the new-fangled tramway, the wonder of the modern age. An iron-wheeled hand cart, once a common sight, is in the foreground. In the distance, once also a common sight, is a mobile workmen's hut. These wooden shelters, like a gypsy caravan, were to be found wherever roadworks and building works were being conducted, taken to the site by steam traction engine. The 'gaffer' seen standing watching the men, no doubt with a pocket watch in his waistcoat pocket, would make his office in the hut, and probably have first dibs at the tea from the kettle permanently on the boil on the coke-fired stove inside.

Above: What a beauty. At Castlecroft this is Mark Miles and Son Ltd's company steam wagon. It is a 'Yorkshire', made in Leeds, probably in 1900. The Yorkshire Patent Steam Wagon Company's first engine was a two cylinder 'compound' with the cylinders mounted one on each side of the chassis; the high pressure on the off side and the low pressure on the near side. The valves were actuated by a single eccentric reversing gear. Sliding gears on the crankshaft driving onto the second motion shaft provided two speeds. In 1906 a new design of engine was introduced which radically altered the layout of the wagon. The engine was now fully enclosed in a cast iron crank case and was mounted vertically between the frames inside the cab. Hackworth valve gear was adopted, and drive to the rear axle was by roller chain. The revised layout had the gearing mounted on an extension of the crankshaft, which allowed 'Yorkshire' to offer three-speed versions of the wagon.

Above: The Aitken Sanatorium in Holcombe closed in 1970. It was subsequently reopened and renamed Darul Uloom Al-Arabiyyah Al-Islamiyyah. Darul Ullom means 'House of Knowledge'. The Sanatorium had first opened its doors in 1910. The Aitken Sanatorium for Consumptives was built to treat folk suffering from 'consumption' as tuberculosis or TB was then known. In the first half of the 20th century TB was a scourge which infected millions of people. Before the advent of effective antibiotics the only potential cure was rest and fresh air. Rich folk sought out mountain air in swish health spas in places such as Switzerland – Bury folk got Holcombe. Thousands of local people down the decades spent months at such local sanatoriums; being kept apart from their families was particularly distressing for children sent there.

Below: Here is a very old photo of the children's ward at Bury General Hospital. Closed when services were transferred to Fairfields, the General Hospital was opened in 1882. The oldest sections of the hospital were the private wards, William Street ward and the board room, which was once a chapel for the dead. Before 1948 and the nationalisation of most hospitals by the creation of the NHS, hospitals were funded by a curious mish-mash of means. Some hospitals were 'poor law' hospitals funded by the ratepayers, while others were 'private' in which patients either paid directly or, more commonly, through various health insurance schemes. But whatever way they were funded all were generally short of cash, hence the annual flag days to raise money. At least here some kind benefactor has donated a rocking horse for the youngsters.

Bottom: The slipper-stitching department of the Bury firm of J H Parker is pictured in 1910. Soles ready to be attached to 'uppers' can be seen stacked up on the benches. Slipper-stitching was clearly 'men's work', with not a woman in sight. Four years later that attitude would rapidly change as thousands of men left their work places to join the armed forces to fight for King and Country against Germany's Kaiser Bill. No doubt as least one of the men here did not live to see 1919. An interesting feature of the scene is the belts taking mechanical power down from overhead shafts, a system little changed from the days of water wheels.

Right: We told you times were hard. These two strapping young mule spinners at the New Victoria Mill, in Wellington Street, pictured here in 1930, can't even afford a pair of clogs for their feet! Well surely there must be some other explanation for having their toes on display, but we can't think what it is. Alas, the sound of looms has long since ceased at the New Victoria. But unlike many other mills at least the building still survives, albeit having had to find other uses and other occupants. Fred Dibnah and his professional colleagues may have changed the Bury skyline forever but at least some parts of our industrial heritage still remain to remind us of what Bury was like half a century ago and more.

Above: A fantastic view taken in the late 1800s looking towards, Joseph Scholes, Stormer Hill Works, in Tottington. The mill chimney dominates the skyline on what is clearly a very windy day. Keen eyed readers may also be able to make out the steam train behind the houses to the right and the man in a boat on the mill pond. The two men in the foreground, on the banking, appear to have spotted the photographer and are posing for the picture.

Top right: Just over a mile outside Bury town centre is the area historically known as Pimhole. Pictured in 1920 is Openshaw's weaving shed, but which Openshaw? James Alfred Openshaw and Brother Ltd or William and George Openshaw Ltd, at their Old Mill? It's a mystery which perhaps only an older reader can resolve. William and George Openshaw, Ltd, of Old Mill, once had 15,648 spindles and 530 looms. All the Openshaws of Bury are descended from John Openshaw, of

Did you know?

Brooksbottom Mill, in Summerseat, which started as a calico printing works in 1773 by the family of Sir Robert Peel marked the beginning of the cotton industry in Bury.

Pimhole, who was born in 1704, and who founded the firm of woollen manufacturers known as John Openshaw and Son and Co. It was the brothers, William and George, who founded the Pimhole cotton mills of William and George Openshaw, in which there were 15,000 spindles and 530 looms. James Alfred Openshaw and Brother Ltd of Pimhole; would boast 80,000 spindles.

Below: Although only boys were admitted to Bury Grammar when the school was founded,

on the re-founding by Roger Kay in 1726 he bequeathed money specifically for girls, the bequest stating: "I charge my Estate called Warth in Ratcliff with the payment of £5 yearly in order that ten poor girls born or to be born in the parish and town of Bury might receive an education....to make them perfect in reading The Bible, to teach them to write well and to be good accountants to fit them for Trades or to be good servants." In 1884, Bury High School for Girls was opened on 22 January as a fee-paying school. The first headmistress was Miss Jane Penelope Kitchener, a cousin of the more famous Lord Kitchener. The school was in Bolton Street, in a building since demolished, on a site opposite the current Leisure Centre. Around 1900, the girls' school's name was changed to Bury Grammar School for Girls. In 1903 the Boys' School moved from The Wylde to half of the current girls' school site.

Did you know?

Less labour due to the Black Death caused ploughed land to become pasture where sheep were then reared - resulting in the start of Bury's woollen industry!

Right: 'Haircut Sir?' If you were in Bell Lane half a century ago you could get your hair trimmed for just sixpence old money (2 1/2p) , and a shave for half that. Well, at least that's what it says on the window frame, though even in 1951 when this photo was taken that was pretty cheap. George Atherton, the proprietor, is modelling the latest salon wear, though his services are far from modern: over the door he advertises razor grinding and setting, as well as the fact that he mends umbrellas. At the bottom of his window he also advertises 'singeing' a service which will be a mystery to younger readers. Singeing involved running a burning taper along the back of the neck after a haircut, supposedly to 'seal' the cut hair. Barbers like this were the despair of fashionable young men; the style choice was invariably short back and sides, or short back and sides.

Below: A picture of the orderly packing room at Halls, in Bury, shows the lines of women packing some of the extensive range of Halls' medicated confectionary products. The only automation appears to be the central conveyor belt, but everything else is done by hand with real diligence and concentration.

Above: There may be no indication of where this photograph was taken, or indeed its exact date, but it is a scene familiar to generations of Bury children. "What are you doing mister?" was the question on every child's lips when strange men with even stranger equipment appeared in their street. Often enough the answer would be no more than "Beggar off" or worse; but sometimes a more sympathetic adult would explain that drains got blocked and that to avoid that happening a trap was installed in every drain hole to catch dirt and rubbish which fell down the grate. The gunge needed sucking out if the drains were not to become clogged. For children the drains were a constant source of fascination, mystery and tearful tragedy – how many pennies have been dropped from small fingers on the way to the sweet shop and disappeared forever?

Right: 'Traffic signals ahead' says the road sign, an important consideration if you've had a few beers. The building opposite is Bury's Crown Brewery pictured in 1964 at a time when most towns had at least one local brewery. One of the last reminders of the Crown Brewery is its name still etched on the window of the Dusty Miller in Crostons Road. October 1967 saw the introduction of the dreaded breathalyzer to Britain's motorists. Before then traffic police used their common sense – could the suspect driver walk in a straight line, stand on one leg, or say 'The Leith Police dismisseth us'? Some say that the breathalyzer was the beginning of the end for the pub trade. In fact increased numbers of motorists made up for the loss of those who lost their licences. It would be the ever-increasing cost of drink and the ban on smoking in the 21st century that did far more damage to the licensed trade.

Above: Wow! What a whopper. We claim no special expertise in matters piscatorial (that's 'fishy things' dressed up in its Sunday best) but our best guess is that giant of a fish is a skate. These two fishmongers in Bury's Princess Street are rightly proud of their monster of the deep, and have made sure the memory of its appearance on their stall is preserved for posterity by having its photograph taken. A fish like this would take an awful lot of chips to go with it; fortunately there are plenty of greengrocers not too far away.

Left: An ambulanceman at Walmersley Road Ambulance Station displaying all the contents of his vehicle for inspection. These days the word ambulanceman, like fireman and policeman, is no longer politically correct, and no doubt the powers-that-be have decreed that the proper term is 'ambulance person'. When this photo was taken, however, we knew what we meant, and ambulance drivers like bus drivers were all still men. Close inspection of the vehicle and the equipment shows this scene to be relatively modern – part of the ever burgeoning NHS ambulance service which began in 1948. Before then ambulances were provided by a variety of agencies, not least the St John Ambulance. The idea of ambulances is just two centuries old, an invention of Napoleon's surgeon for moving battlefield casualties.

Wallwork - Heat Treatment Specialists

Metal processing and engineering has long been associated with Bury, so when Wallwork Heat Treatment were looking for new premises in 1979, Lodge Bank Works on Lord Street made an ideal new home. The buildings had originally been used by Bentley and Jackson (founded 1860) to manufacture paper making machinery and afforded the good headroom and overhead cranes that Wallwork was seeking to install large heat treatment furnaces.

The company was founded by Robert Wallwork in 1959. The Wallwork family had a long history of being involved in engineering in Manchester, including the operation of a large foundry in Red Bank, Manchester. Initially, Wallwork Heat Treatment had premises in Mersey Square, Stockport, and then Knowl Street, in Stalybridge, before the move to Bury.

The original Lodge Bank Works chimney bearing the lettering 'B&J 1878' was eventually demolished in the late 1980s.

The company carries out heat treatment of metal components for manufacturing industry, anything from kitchen knives to large gears for marine gearboxes and more recently has specialised in processing aircraft components and aero engine parts.

Wallwork has operated a fleet of distinctive bright green trucks since the mid-1970s (long before Asda started to use the colour)

in those days the paint was specially mixed and Robert Wallwork painted the vehicles by hand with a brush! Now operating over 40 trucks, the company is well identified by their distinctive green livery.

The company expanded with sites in Birmingham (1989) and Cambridge (1997). Owing to the lack of suitable premises in Cambridge, Wallwork purchased a field and contracted Peel Construction from Ramsbottom to build the new factory.

Wallwork purchased another site on the opposite side of Rochdale Road, on Back Derby Street (now Derby way), in the mid-1990s. The building which was formally used by Bury Council and NORWEB is believed to have been originally owned by the Bury Co-operative Brewing and Distilling Co. Ltd (1861) who also owned the Robin Hood Pub at that time. It is now used to house Wallwork Cast Alloys, which is the only working foundry remaining in Bury.

Further expansion in 2005 saw Wallwork purchase the ex-Wheeler Tubes site on Hacking Street, which has now become the group head office.

Now employing 100 people at their head office in Bury and 240 people nationwide, Wallwork it is the second largest heat treatment company in the UK.

*Top left: Founder, Robert Wallwork (1923-2001). **Above left:** Preparing to install equipment at the Lord Street works in 1979. **Above:** Construction of the company's Cambridge site. **Below:** Part of the Wallwork fleet outside their Lord Street premises, 2011.*

Antler Ltd - A Very Special Case

Antler Ltd is a proud British company with a reputation built on over almost a century of luggage-making experience, leading the way in quality, innovation and design.

The company has a long and established tradition of producing luggage designed for lightness and strength without compromising quality.

Based at its headquarters in Alfred Street, Bury, Antler's in-house design team is constantly working to produce new styles and designs to make the British luggage market the envy of the world.

The Antler story began in 1865 when John Boultbee Brooks left his hometown of Hinckley, in Leicestershire, with £20 in his pocket. According to company legend it was in that year that the young man, then 19-years old, bought himself a new-fangled velocipede. He would have cut quite a dashing figure, but that was not all he cut; the wooden saddle was excruciatingly uncomfortable. His father made leather saddles for horses - and indeed he and his contemporaries, normally came to work on a horse. So the young John set about designing and developing a comfortable saddle from leather in his father's works.

John Boultbee Brooks (1846-1921) established a works in Great Charles Street, Birmingham, for the manufacture of leather strapping for horse harnesses and general leather goods. In 1870, noting that more and more people were indulging in the new pastime of cycling, Brooks went over to the manufacture of bicycle saddles.

The first modern-looking 'safety' bicycle came on the scene in 1880, and with it the need for more comfortable saddles. No longer were riders willing to accept that the only option was to sit astride a piece of formed wood.

Above: *Early Brooks Saddle bags.* **Below:** *An early 20th century photograph of staff and management at Brooks with their products of the time.*

In 1882 Brooks filed a patent for his world-famous sprung bicycle saddle, the first of its kind. After that he went on to file a number of patents for bicycle saddles, motor cycle saddles and other leather goods. These included galoshes, snap-on leggings, handlebar muffs, folding footrests, toe-straps, gents and ladies cycling shoes, oil-skin clothing and, of course, bags.

Many of these items are still in existence and can be found in cycling museums throughout Britain and the world.

A little known fact, however, is that Brooks' also manufactured furniture – chairs, tables, desks, cabinets and mirrors for home, hotel or business use and stools, lockers, cupboards, bins, shelves and tables for commercial and industrial use.

By the early 1900s the firm was offering an astonishingly broad range of bicycle saddles and other leather accessories such as saddle bags, tool bags, saddle back rests, inner tube cases, motorcycle belt cases, pannier bags, luggage bags, hat cases and even bicycle-mounted cigar trays.

The firm became a limited company in 1914.

Then came the Stag and Antler brand of products as J Boultbee Brook's son entered the passenger luggage market with leather wardrobe trunks for ocean liners and unique 'motor trunks' attached to cars. A keen interest in wildlife led to the adoption of the stag's head and antler as a brand symbol for the luggage line.

Generally hide luggage was made over a timber frame, often of oak or mahogany but generally pine. This timber framework was sometimes externalised, resulting in 'wood banded' or 'hooped' luggage.

These wooden banded cases were often interspersed with

*Top left and top right: A Brooks Saddles truck demonstrates the quality and strength of Antler luggage in the 1960s. **Above:** The Stag and Antler branding of the 1920s. **Left:** A J.B. Brooks & Co. Ltd. exhibition stand showcasing Antler luggage.*

brown or green canvas and, occasionally, leather. Some larger trunks were constituted over a wicker foundation.

Generally cases were made of cowhide, of many varieties of grade and thickness. The highest quality leather used in case manufacture was Connolly Leather.

Prior to practical use leather has to undergo 'tanning', which involves the leather being stripped of both its external and internal layers, leaving the central layer, called 'derma'.

There was a period when white luggage was popular. This clean looking and glamorous luggage was generally made from bleached cowhide. Goat, sheep, pigskin and synthetic material were also sometimes used. Vulcanised fibres and compressed vegetable fibres were also common.

The interior of luggage revealed much about the quality and ownership of the case. Early cases might be lined with dark green, deep blue or black Morocco leather, whilst later models might have a purple or striped ticking lining, silk, velvet or plain canvas.

Paper linings, or water-marked paper lining were also used, as well as synthetic materials such as rexine. Often fabric-lined cases had bunched pockets to secure loose items.

The luxury end of the market would be a dressing case, for both men and women, fitted with lidded bottles and various dressing equipment, sometimes fitted with silver or even gold fittings.

During the 1930s the Stag and Antler division of Brooks invented the first soft top suitcase – top and bottom wire frame covered with patent leather or Vynide. Legend has it that Harrods sold the first consignment in a single day.

Just before the Second World War the Company began to diversify and bought a company called Brookes Engineering. That, as the name implies was an engineering company manufacturing components for the cycle and car trades. They also bought a Company called Evertaut Limited, which was entirely devoted to the manufacture of industrial shelving, office furniture and industrial seating.

Top right and left: Production of Antler luggage in the 1960s. *Centre:* 1950s advertising using the latest film of the day with a fitting slogan: 'Luggage for Your Honeymoon should be Antler' was advertised alongside 'Father of the Bride' starring Elizabeth Taylor and Spencer Tracy. And alongside the 1952 film 'Lovely to Look At', starring Kathryn Grayson and Howard Keel, was 'Ask for Antler Soft Top Cases'.

During the Second World War Brooks' Antler shifted its focus to producing haversacks, webbing belts and similar military equipment to help in the war effort.

After the war there was a return to the luggage business, with further innovation in soft-sided luggage with rich, quality linings. The Company now took over English Rose Kitchens, manufacturers of steel and wood kitchen furniture. Later, the Company also took over Foxcroft Luggage Limited, a travel goods company catering for the lower priced luggage market.

J. B. Brooks Industries was now formed, as a holding company for the whole Group.

A new age of mass air travel dawned in the 1950s, and tourism boomed. Antler saw further opportunities to develop products to cater for a new and ever-expanding market. One best seller, the 'Airstream' combined soft and hard fabrics into one suitcase. Whatever way people travelled, Antler led the field with technical innovations.

In 1958 the Brooks saddle division was sold to Raleigh, and Antler subsequently joined the Harris & Sheldon Group, a leading conglomerate headed by John Miller, who later became Chairman of Antler.

Due to the redevelopment of Birmingham the Company was compelled to leave its premises, still in Great Charles Street, and as Government policy at that time was that no Industrial development certificates would be available to any company in the Birmingham area, the business moved to Bury in 1962. There it re-established itself in the Pilot Works, in Alfred Street, where it incorporated production of both Foxcroft and Antler top quality travel goods and lower priced luggage.

Additional manufacturing sites were also established in Mossley, Littleborough and Exeter to match increasing demand, not least for fibre-board mould cases for Marks & Spencer.

By the mid-1960s the firm was employing some 400 workers, equally male and female. Exports were going as far afield as Singapore and Japan. Materials were sourced almost entirely from the UK, with a small proportion imported from Sweden.

Aluminium framed cases and zip cases were developed in the 1970s; moulded fibreboard, however, remained the mainstay of

Top left and top right: The company's former Foxcroft, Littleborough, site. *Centre:* Antler's best selling 'Airstream' luggage. *Left:* Antler's Pilot Works, Alfred Street, head office in the 1960s.

The company 'went public' for the first time in 1986 - with Jim Miller retaining 40 per cent of the shares. Three years later, in 1989, all the equity in the business was purchased by the Wassall Group, a conglomerate headed by John Miller's son Chris.

During the mid-1980s Antler dramatically expanded its business: annual sales rose from £4 million to £11 million, with new ranges and an expansion of the core 'Traveller' range. Trolley cases, too, were introduced, followed by rapid growth in both soft luggage and hard sided luggage.

Towards the end of the 20th Century, Antler continued to forge ahead with new products, entering the hard luggage suitcase market and introducing new quality leather goods. The company played a key part in the roller case revolution, a technical innovation that changed the way luggage was shaped forever.

business until sales of zip cases began to become substantial in the late 1970s. The pace of change accelerated in 1974 when Antler acquired the Revelation brand and the Exeter factory of Kingfisher Luggage following the demise of the British Luggage Group.

In the 1980s Antler became the last British luggage manufacturer of any size as an increasing flood of imports led to the contraction of British manufacture. Department stores began retailing imported luggage including leather briefcases. Meanwhile, demand for soft sided luggage over fibreboard continued to increase.

Antler responded to the market challenges by establishing its Carry Care Division, providing tailor-made carrying cases for samples, computer software, tools and special equipment.

Today Antler's global market is growing at a rapid pace, and the firm is investing to take advantage of the keen interest from overseas markets. Antler is the best selling luggage brand in Australia and is growing rapidly in other key markets including Japan, Canada, and South Korea. Antler products are sold in more than 39 countries around the world.

Some of Antler's best selling products include Liquis, Antler's lightest hard case ever with a distinctive rippled exterior inspired by waves of tumbling water and also Which? 2011 Best Buy-winning New Size Zero and Duolite, both ultra lightweight and packed with innovations such as silent glide wheels and aluminum trolley systems In 2010 the business was bought out by LDC, the

Top left: Members of the 1968 British Olympic team leaving for Mexico with their Airzip cases made by Antler. *Centre:* Antler's elegant 1970s 'Bond Street' range. *Left:* Former World's Strongest Man Geoff Capes testing Antlers revolutionary new 'Cordura' fabric . *Top right:* Ex-Formula 1 World Champion, Nigel Mansell, loading his Bond St luggage.

David says "Our plan is to grow overseas revenues considerably over the next three to five years, including targeting Germany and Scandinavia for the first time.

"We are focused on developing an independent retailer network in the US, and see developing countries including China, India, Brazil and Korea as a huge opportunity.

What next for Antler? In the 21st century, Antler Ltd continues to innovate, building upon its unique heritage that has continually embraced and pioneered new developments in the luggage industry, making the Antler brand the choice for quality, strength and technical innovation.

private equity arm of Lloyds Banking Group. LDC appointed 47-year-old father-of-two David Benjamin as the new Chief Executive.

He says: "I thought it was a great opportunity. Antler is an iconic British brand".

David began to display a strong business pedigree from an early age. As a child in Warwickshire he bought chickens and tended a vegetable patch, earning extra pocket money by selling the produce.

At 18, he took a job at a local department store progressing to managing its glass and china department.

After a spell running two independent china shops, David's next move was to another iconic British manufacturer, Royal Worcester and Spode, where he spent 23 years working his way up to group managing director.

At Antler he is excited about looking overseas to accelerate Antler's growth, with plans to tailor the range to foreign tastes and broaden its distribution.

Top left: An Australian tram carrying advertising for Antler Duolite and Liquis. *Bottom left:* Advertising Antler World Class Luggage in Dubai. *Left:* From left to right, Antler's Duolite, Purelite and Liquis luggage. *Below:* David Benjamin, CEO of Antler, 2011(MEN Media).

Holy Cross College - Handing on the light

The College now known as Holy Cross, formerly Bury Convent, has changed and developed a great deal since it was founded in 1878.

Let us take you back to Germany and the Kulturkampf of the 19th Century. At the same time as Otto von Bismarck was trying to get rid of teachers who were religiously inclined, Cardinal Vaughan of the Salford Diocese was searching for them. The Congregation of the Daughters of the Cross had been founded by Blessed Marie Thérèse Haze in Liège, Belgium in 1833 and by 1851 had extended to Germany. But the

sisters who had been welcome in Germany until that point now found themselves banished. By happy coincidence, Cardinal Vaughan's search was underway and some of those same sisters, who were running a school in Dusseldorf, found themselves invited to Bury. None of this was easy for them though: on arrival in 1878 they were without even such bare necessities such as chairs and tables and cups and saucers. However, by dint of starting a small school and charging pupils a penny a week, as well as recruiting assistance from the people of Bury, they were able to gather together the essentials. The cramped conditions in a little house in Bank Street necessitated a move to Derby House, further down Manchester Road, and very soon another move further down again to The Ferns, a building which remains a key part of the Summerfield Building of the present College.

Education for all was a relatively new idea in those days, and as the Sisters expanded their property new demands were made on them, including that of training of pupil teachers. As these trainees came from other parts of the country and from Ireland, they needed a place to live: so the need for accommodation grew. Along the way a very beautiful Chapel, described as 'Puginesque' by some and a gem of its kind, was built on the lines of the Mother House chapel in Rue Hors-Château in Liège. Problems with inadequate foundations led to its eventual demolition, with a temporary chapel being located elsewhere. On the site the brand new Maureen Haverty building was erected but – like many of the college buildings – it was

Above: *A school trip to Ashworth Valley in 1883.*
Below: *Students pose for a photograph in 1900.*

finally Holy Cross Sixth Form College. Sister had a dream that she might have a little college on site for the training of good teachers, quite separate from the pupil teacher programme of the time. In 1999 her dream would at last become a reality when, in conjunction with Liverpool Hope University, adult provision at last arrived at the College, including BA, BSc and MA degrees, and PGCEs, helping prepare many people for a career in the world of education and elsewhere. This development is known as the University Centre.

Another idea that would come full circle is the name. The foundation stone of the Holy Cross School was laid back in 1887 in the Golden Jubilee of Queen Victoria's reign. Other names would be used in subsequent decades, but in 1979, when the

sympathetically designed to reflect the brick and stone and low Belgian-style 'mansard' roofs of earlier wings. (Sister Maureen was a much-loved RE teacher at the College who died in 1993.) In 2012, however, plans are afoot for a new building on a site just south of the College, which will include a new Chapel. It is hoped that the original altar, remembered by many former students, will form a part of the new design.

Top: A Classroom in 1907. **Above left:** *An early 20th century dormitory.* **Below:** *The school Art Room, 1935.*

Back in the 1870s, however, Sister Iphigenie was the driving force behind all that happened in the early days at Bury Convent. At first she and her sisters worked in the parish school of St Marie's, but soon a secondary school was born, which eventually became Bury Convent Grammar School and

present form of the College was being finalised, the title Holy Cross College was the one that found universal favour. It reflects the vision of the Cross that Blessed Marie Thérèse experienced in the early days of the order, and which is commemorated in the symbol of the College and of the Daughters of the Cross – the cross surmounted by a ring or 'corona' of light.

It was in 1905 that the school ceased to be a public elementary school and began work as a secondary school: the preparatory school for the younger pupils then functioned separately. The secondary school was entitled to grants from the Board of Education. Money was obtained from various other sources and

buildings erected about that time are still in use today – including the 'Tower'. In 1910, however, a great fire damaged the boarding school at the top and back of Summerfield, adjacent to The Ferns. Records tell us that the rebuilding and refurbishment costs were £500. Grants became available over the years enabling further improvement. The sixth form started in 1920, followed by the purchase of Agincourt in 1922 and the playing fields next door soon after. Agincourt has now been demolished making way for the Marie Thérèse building opened at Christmas 2004, whilst part of the playing fields made way for yet another new building, named after Sister Mary Kelly and opened in 2001. Sister Mary was Principal (twice) and Provincial of the Daughters of the Cross in this country. Until shortly before she died in 2008 she was still active in the College she loved, in the Chaplaincy and on the Governing Body.

Lest this became a litany of buildings and money, we should pause for a moment to think of the enormous human benefit that has resulted from all these efforts.

Holy Cross has been fortunate in the wonderful headteachers, teachers, support staff, governors and principals who have served the school over the years. They have

Top: *The Emilie Mary Building pictured in 1952.* **Left:** *The original college chapel.*

use today, albeit with a new roof, new windows and new, attractive cladding fitted in 2011. The sixth form that started with single figures in the early 1920s grew to between two and three hundred. The school roll shot up to over seven hundred.

Yet further major changes were soon on the horizon. In the late 1970s the Government decided that direct grant schools were no longer an option. Three choices were available: the school could close, it could go 'independent' or, thirdly, join forces with the Local Authority as part of a planned reorganization into a 'tertiary' system in the borough, when all schools would become 11-16, with a Further Education College and a Sixth Form College for post-16 students. The school authorities chose the latter option and so far have not regretted it. The outcome of all the discussions on reorganisation was that the school would become an open-access co-educational Sixth Form College. It was felt, however, that the young men who came to the college would not want to admit that they attended a Convent establishment so a new name was needed. It took little deliberation to decide to revert to the original name of Holy Cross College.

enriched the lives of scores of pupils and students and staff and made Bury a better place by their presence and effort. The religious significance of their lives of service has added to the growth in spirituality of hundreds of people. In all its successes the school and College have held on firmly to these truths and the beauty of our mottos: Omnis scientia vera est a Deo - 'All true knowledge comes from God' – and In hoc signo vinces – ' In this sign you will conquer'. (The latter is, of course, a reference to the sign and way of the Cross, and reflects the great vision of Constantine in 312 AD which seemed to repeat itself in a certain way at the foundation of the Daughters of the Cross.)

Readers who attended the school in the 1930s may recall 'the year of three kings'. The year 1936 began with pupils mourning the death of King George V then celebrating the proclamation of another King Edward VIII, trying to make sense of his abdication, and eventually celebrating the Coronation of King George VI and Queen Elizabeth.

And if the abdication crisis was not enough to puzzle young minds what of war with all its scares, tribulations and deprivations? Those in charge of the school simply looked ahead and worked out an elaborate and imaginative building programme that would be put in place when peace returned. In 1944 Holy Cross became a Direct Grant School, known as Bury Convent Grammar School. When the war ended in 1945 numbers began to increase.

The Boarding School closed in 1950 to make room for the rapidly expanding day school. The long-awaited building programme swung into action and has not ceased since. The Emilie Mary building erected in the 1950s (and named after Sister Emilie Mary, a former headmistress) is still in

In 1993 the Government decided that a body called the Further Education Funding Council should take over responsibility for post-16 colleges. Effectively, the College was now out of

Top left: School leavers of 1973. **Centre:** *The new Holy Cross emblem.* **Below:** *The entrance to Bury Convent Grammar School.*

the control of the Local Education Authority and was 'incorporated' – becoming a corporation in its own right. Holy Cross's new funding masters, the Further Education Funding Council, were far from overly generous. The simple fact was that the College did not have enough money and it had a few hard years. Since funding was historically based, the well-off local authorities did well, but Bury had to wait for 'convergence' which came in over a few years. Without the generosity of the Daughters of the Cross at this point, not least in funding a major building programme, the College's progress would not have been so dramatic. Happily a different funding body - the Learning and Skills Council - eventually came in to look after the College and money came in from several different sources, including the Daughters of the Cross and the students' own fund raising efforts as well as excellent financial management and stewardship, sending the College well on its way to enjoying well-deserved state of the art facilities.

There was a time when 700 girls aged 11-18 seemed to be the maximum for the campus: today there are approximately 2000 students aged 16-19. But that is not all: there are many people in our area who, for one reason or another, left formal education early but who would

now like to return to it; Holy Cross has the facilities to help them do so. In conjunction with Liverpool Hope University, Holy Cross decided to use slack periods such as evenings to provide degree, diploma or other forms of extended education. That initiative flourished and now more than 600 local people are taking advantage of the courses every year. The core partnership with Hope has extended to Edge Hill University and Leeds Metropolitan University, and to the Catholic University College in Twickenham that the Pope visited when he came to Britain in 2010 – St Mary's, Strawberry Hill. As mentioned before the Holy Cross University Centre offers full honours degrees entirely taught in Bury, and 'top ups' for those who have foundation degrees. Despite a later start in many cases, and less conventional routes into higher education, our students gain an exceptionally high number of first class and 2:1 degrees.

The Sixth Form side of the College also now rejoices in the fact that it has been placed among the top sixth form colleges in the country and has been awarded Beacon Status. It is regularly in the top ten nationally for results, especially for A* and A

Top: University Centre students graduating.
Left: Statue of Our Lady from the present Chapel.

grades, and was recently second in the country for Success Rates. Many former students have gone on to Oxford, Cambridge and other excellent universities, as well as making names for themselves around the world in interesting careers.

None of the developments which have taken place down the years however could have happened without the courage and bravery of those first Sisters who arrived in Bury with Sister Iphigenie in 1878. Now that a new building is being developed adjacent to the historic site (on land which once belonged to the Daughters of the Cross and sheltered the Sixth Form House) perhaps it will be named after her example (although it is true that we already have an Iphigenie Sports Hall – the only Sports Hall we know on the second floor of a college –

built on stilts as a testimony to the coziness of our site!) In the fullness of time those sisters' places were taken by devoted successors who have appreciated the mission of the Founders and built on the spiritual ethos they passed down. That mission and ethos is still palpable today. It is perhaps the greatest reason why students and staff feel so happy here and why Holy Cross is such a strong community, attracting students and staff from far and wide. Whatever the future may hold today's staff are well aware that they are the custodians of a precious inheritance and their task is to keep that torch alight, and in their turn, too, to pass it on.

Above: A Level students celebrating on results day. Below: Holy Cross reception area.

Printpack - A Family To Be Proud Of

There can't be many businesses operating in Bury that are part of a multi-national business with over a billion dollars a year turnover. Nor can there be many businesses which can claim a history of going back almost three centuries. Yet today's Printpack Enterprises Ltd, the packaging firm based in Bridge Hall Mills, can place a tick in both boxes.

Printpack, now firmly focused on flexible packing, has multiple manufacturing plants in North America, Mexico and Europe. The headquarters of the European business is in Bury, with another plant in Saffron Walden, in Essex.

The Bury operation supplies high quality printed flexible packaging for wrapping crisps, snacks, biscuits, confectionery and for labelling carbonated soft drinks bottles. Main customers are major food and beverage manufacturers such as Walkers Crisps, KP Foods, McVities, Burtons Biscuits, Coca Cola, Fox's Biscuits, Cadbury and Nestle.

Packaging has been the foundation of a number of fortunes in the 20th century. For younger readers, buying food in printed packages is the normal way that food is supplied: but things were not always so. Until the 1950s and 60s it was still commonplace to have food of all kinds displayed loose, weighed out and then put into a brown paper bag.

Today food of almost all kinds is pre-packed. It was the advent of the supermarket which spurred the change in packaging. Brown paper bags were out and in came cellophane and plastic.

*Top: An aerial view of Bridge Hall Mills, 1924. **Left:** James Erskine Love Jr, founder of Printpack. **Below:** Bridge Hall Mills in the 18th century.*

The fledgling new business was beginning to find its feet by 1930, a position which all too soon would be undermined by the years of economic recession. Though the outbreak of war in 1939 would inevitably see a further fall in production as raw materials became scarce, the Bridge Hall Mills remained fully occupied as contracts for war work came in. Some 200,000 square feet of factory space would be given over to war production. Contracts were received at the mills for the manufacturing of cartridge containers: by February 1942 work began on building the gluing, winding and cutting machines to

And yet this story of one the world's most successful purveyors of plastic packaging begins with paper.

Paper-making had begun at Bury's Bridge Hall Mills in the early 1700s. In the 19th century Bridge Hall Mills was one of the largest paper mills in Britain, but paper making was first recorded there as early as 1716.

A large mill complex grew under the ownership of George Wrigley & Son during the 19th century. At its height in the 1880s the factory employed almost 500 local folk.

Sadly, the good times could not last and the paper mill closed in 1924 - apparently forever.

The origins of the present day flexible packaging manufacturing by Printpack can be traced to the Transparent Paper Company in the 1920s. 'TP' Ltd, or 'Tranny' as the firm was known locally, started the process of manufacturing cellulose film (clear paper) at Bridge Hall Mills in Bury, in 1928. The freehold of the Mills was bought by Transparent Paper on 30 April, 1928, for £65,000, and new machinery was soon installed to manufacture acetate film or 'cellophane', the latter name, incidentally, being a trademark which had been registered by its inventor, Swiss chemist, J E Brandenburger, in 1908.

Acetate film was manufactured from a compound of cellulose and acetic acid and technically known as acetyl-cellulose or cellulose acetate. A new acetate plant was erected during 1929 and production finally got underway that autumn. Acetate was, however, relatively expensive to produce and production would very soon shift to the cheaper viscose film.

produce those tubular cardboard cartons. By the end of the war over six million containers had been produced.

The cardboard tube business would continue after the war, with the Tubular Case and Carton Company being created as a subsidiary of Transparent Paper Ltd. Expansion would come in the post war world.

Top left: *A derelict Bridge Hall Mill in 1928.* **Above:** *Inside the Slitting Department in the 1930s.* **Below:** *Transparent Paper Ltd, circa 1930s.*

In late 1944 part of the mills had been destroyed by fire. Though little had changed at the mills since 1915 a new finishing section was completed in 1947. A programme of new building and investment in equipment would continue over the next ten years. Investment between 1954 and 1956 would double the plant's capacity.

To improve its sales of 'cello', TP Ltd now started to 'convert' or print on the film with the construction of the conversion plant in the 1950s - this would be the basis of the current business which in the post war years would grow dramatically from having some 450 employees in 1956 to a peak of some 1,600 in 1960.

In those days the manufacture of cellulose film was a rather smelly process due to the chemicals used, something many readers may recall. Happily, by contrast, manufacturing today is odour free, with no impact on the local environment.

Cellophane started to be replaced by plastic in the 1970s. The world-wide decline in demand for cellophane resulted in the closure of the cello plant on 1982.

Polythene made its first appearance at Bridge Hall Mills in the early 1950s when Transparent Paper created a subsidiary, Flexible Packaging Ltd, to develop and sell this new product, though it soon sold it off as unprofitable.

Two decades later, however, the focus of Transparent Paper would shift back to the printing and conversion of flexible plastic packaging. Following the closure of the cello plant in 1982 the business passed through the hands of a number of different owners in the 1980s and early 1990s. In 1993 it was

Top: Production of jettison fuel tanks during the years of the Second World War. Above: Post war view inside the Slitting Department. Far left: Maintaining the film rollers. Centre left: State-of-the-art design at Printpack. Left: Quality control. Printpack have a determination to settle for nothing less than the highest quality.

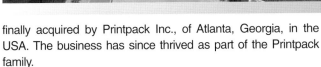

finally acquired by Printpack Inc., of Atlanta, Georgia, in the USA. The business has since thrived as part of the Printpack family.

The Printpack group was founded in Atlanta by James Erskine Love Jr in 1956. It remains privately owned by the Love family, headed by Erskine's eldest son Dennis as Company President.

In order to get his small firm afloat back in the mid-1950s Erskine had used every available asset he possessed: equity in his home, his car and even the surrender value of his life insurance. He did not possess a single dollar which was not put into the business. Then, with an equal amount of money - $60,000 - borrowed from the bank, he started the business with his wife and his father. Producing cellophane wrappers, and soon afterwards printing those same wrappers, would prove to be an astonishingly shrewd move.

At the start, Erskine Love was his company's sole employee, though soon John Sample, blind in one eye, and as a result rejected by the Bell Telephone company, joined Erskine. By March 1957 Erskine was advising the bank that he expected to be able to pay off the loan within weeks. The number of employees grew to ten. In that first full year sales amounted to $26,000, by 1959 the company had an annual turnover of $1,300,000, a year later that had grown by a further half million dollars; that expansion would continue for thirty and more years, and in due course lead to Bury.

Erskine Love died in 1987 aged just 59; he had lived to see his once small company become an industry giant. All five of Erskine Love's sons, however, would be involved in the business. In the UK Erskine's fourth son, Bill, was Sales and Marketing Director for five years prior to his tragic death at the age of just 41when his plane crashed into Mount Kenya in Africa in 2003. His wife, daughter and nine other family members also died.

Today, global turnover is approaching $1.5billion with ambitions to get to $2billion by 2017.

In 2009, the company opened a plant in China and is in the process of increasing its capability. Opportunities are also being explored in India.

A second business in Mexico has been acquired, doubling the size of the existing business there and providing a platform to grow Latin American sales.

In the US the group has moved to a new $10million Corporate Headquarters in Atlanta, and has recently built a new plant in Bloomington, Indiana.

The main change to the European business is the $50million investment in a new plant in Kutno, Poland. This offers additional capability to strengthen European business and allow Printpack to develop new markets. That investment is expected to help the company grow its European business from about £70million to almost £100million between 2011 and 2017.

Top left, top right and above: Printpack's new plant in Kutno, Poland. *Below:* A bird's eye view of Prinpack's Bridge Hall Mills, Bury, site.

Bury College - Supporting Learners

Market Street in Bury is home to one of the most respected and outstanding colleges of further education in the country.

Bury College opened as a tertiary college on 1 September, 1987, as a result of Bury MBC's decision to develop a tertiary education system for Bury. The College was formed by the merger of the then Bury College of Further Education with premises in Bury and Radcliffe; Peel Sixth Form College located off Market Street, Bury; Stand Sixth Form College in Whitefield; and a number of Youth Training Scheme (YTS) Units located in various parts of the Metropolitan Borough.

Each of the main constituents, i.e. Bury College of Further Education, Peel Sixth Form College and Stand Sixth Form College, had very different origins and histories.

Bury College of Further Education started life as Bury Technical College (or "Bury Tech" as it was referred to colloquially) and was built on land adjacent to the original Market Hall and Open Market in the centre of Bury. Construction of the College building

at the junction of Market Street and what is now Angouleme Way took place during the 1930s when it was designed to house courses that included Textile Manufacturing, Shoe Making, Shorthand and Typing, Engineering and Construction. The later addition of a papermaking plant meant that Bury College was one of only two in England to offer courses to operatives from the paper and board industry. This reflected the strong manufacturing base that the industry had in the Bury area for many years.

From May 1940 to May 1946 Bury Technical College was occupied by the Royal Military College of Science (Fire Control Wing) to provide specialist courses in the use of fire control instruments during the Second World War.

Pupils from the Technical College became part of the first cohort of pupils at The Derby School, off Radcliffe Road, Bury, which opened as a Grammar/Technical School on 1 September 1959. Another major component of the initial intake to the Derby School was the pupils from Bury High

Top left: The Woodbury Centre, 2011. Left: A Stand Grammar School souvenir from the formal opening of the of new building in 1913.

Below: Staff and pupils of Stand Grammar School pictured on 28 June, 1913.

School, later to be Wellington Secondary School, which was located on the site off Market Street. Reorganisation of Secondary Education by the borough in 1979 saw the site that was bordered by Market Street, Wellington Road and Parliament Street become a sixth form centre for the north of the borough; the Peel Sixth Form College.

Following the Local Authority's review of Post-16 Education after Local Government Reorganisation in 1974, Bury College of Further Education, as the Technical College was then named, merged with Radcliffe Technical College to form the Bury Metropolitan College of Further Education. The College vacated its premises in Whittaker Street, Bank House, the Town Hall in Radcliffe and the Hope Park Annexe in Prestwich in 1986. At that point courses in areas such as Catering, Art & Design, Nursery Nursing, Management and Supervisory Studies transferred to refurbished accommodation at the former Whitefield High School, off Albert Road, Whitefield.

The 1979 reorganisation of Secondary Education in Bury established Stand Sixth Form College as the sixth form centre for the south of the borough. Stand Sixth Form College was located on seven acres of land in Church Lane, Whitefield. The purchase of the site had been approved in January 1908 when Lancashire Education Committee bought it from the Earl of Derby to house Stand School and its playing fields. The school was originally founded in 1688 under the will of Henry Siddall and had close connections with the Unitarian Chapel in Ringley Road, Whitefield. By 1900, Stand School, with 60 boys and several Masters- including science and art masters and a drill sergeant- had already encountered financial difficulties and Lancashire Education Committee took it over in 1908. Alderman J R Ragdale, who was then Chairman of the School's Governors, opened the new school on September 6, 1913. The School then grew from a handful of boys to a mixed school of 400 pupils when he retired in 1917.

George Longman was the Head Teacher when the School moved to the new building in Church Lane. Mr Longman devised the school motto "sto ut serviam",

which is Latin for 'I stand to serve'. A distinguished former pupil of the School was Robert Clive, who became Lord Clive of Plassey. Major General Clive was a soldier who helped establish British military and political supremacy in India in the 18th century. The School catered for both boys and girls until 1937 when the new girls' school opened in Higher Lane. The boys' school continued to develop with 700 pupils on roll and the building became Stand Sixth Form College in 1979 and part of Bury College in 1987.

Bury College was incorporated on 1 April, 1993, under the Further and Higher Education Act 1992 and governors then commenced on the major strategy of developing provision on the town centre campus in Bury. This meant the gradual phasing out of the use of premises in other parts of the borough. The proceeds from the sale of the former Whitefield High School and Stand Sixth Form College sites were used to fund major

Left: John Ragdale, Chairman of Governors in 1913. **Top right:** *A Stand Grammar Memorial Plaque for former students who lost their lives in the Second World War.* **Below:** *An early illustration of Stand Grammar School.*

developments at the College's Woodbury Centre (the renamed College building on Market Street) and on the former Peel Sixth Form College site.

The past decade has seen on-going major investment in state of the art facilities for Bury College learners and staff. The Millennium Centre opened in September, 2000, and was part funded by the sale of the former Stand Sixth Form College site.

Other developments have included the construction of the Beacon Centre, the Prospects Centre, the Innovation Centre and the Aspire Centre as new builds and the acquisition of the Enterprise Centre (formerly the 'Bury Times' building) on Market Street. There have also been major refurbishments at the Woodbury Centre.

Originally the Woodbury Centre building housed a swimming pool that was used by students and staff and was also used as a base for swimming lessons for pupils from primary schools in Bury.

The pool area was subsequently redeveloped to provide the popular 3CZons Restaurant- an industry-standard kitchen and restaurant used to train the chefs and hospitality staff of the future.

The original main hall with its stage and balcony (subsequently converted to provide students' refectory and classrooms) housed numerous community events ranging from the Bury Horticultural Society flower shows to drama and musical stage shows by local societies.

The former College playing field at the junction of Market Street and Wellington Road was subsequently developed to provide the multi-purpose athletics facility that exists today.

The College is now able to boast new facilities for engineering courses, state-of-the-art IT suites and computer aided design studios. Continuing investment in facilities is taking place in 2011/2012 with a new build for construction. Further refurbishment and developments at the Woodbury Centre will provide a new learning resource centre and library, industry standard art studios, a new outdoor courtyard to increase social space, state-of-the-art classrooms and the latest in IT technology.

Top left: Office Studies in 1971. **Left:** *Department of Science and General Education, 1974.* **Above:** *Bury College library in the 1970s.* **Below:** *The department of Business and General Studies in the 1970s.*

The success of Bury College today can be measured by its excellent provision and success rates of learners. The College's reputation and popularity can be seen by the growth in the number of students since the inception of the College in 1987. The total number of 16+ students who enrolled on full-time courses in 1984 at the then Bury College of Further Education, Peel College and Stand College was 1019. The number of full-time students currently enrolled in 2011 is over 4,300.

In recognition of the high standards at Bury College in 2007 the College was awarded Outstanding in all areas by the government's Ofsted inspectors. Inspectors praised in particular: "Very high success rates for learners aged 16-18" and "Outstanding quality of provision". In 2011, government Data Authority figures showed that Bury College was the highest performing Further Education College in Greater Manchester.

Top left: *Market Street Centre of Bury College under construction.* **Above:** *Piazza development, 2011.* **Below:** *A 2011 aerial view of the Bury College Millennium Centre campus.*

D.G. Steel & Son Engineering Ltd
Geared for Progress

Despite the much publicised general decline in the manufacturing sector, particularly engineering, D.G.Steel & Son Engineering Ltd. - a relative newcomer to Bury - has rather 'bucked the trend' in its continuous and steady growth as an engineering company specialising in industrial gear manufacture since its establishment in 1970 .

The company was founded by Dennis Steel (D.G.Steel) in May 1970.

Born in 1921 in Oldham, Dennis in common with a large proportion of the male population of the town, served an apprenticeship at Platt Brothers (at the time the worlds' leading Textile Machinery manufacturer).This lead to his promotion at 17 into the drawing office and at 20 becoming the manager of an engineering workshop of some 300 machinists producing a multitude of parts vital to the war effort.

In peace-time his experience lead to him becoming General Manager and subsequently Managing Director of the Engineering Division of Carrington & Dewhurst - a leading Lancashire textile yarns producer.

The mid to late 1960s saw the further demise of textile machinery manufacture in England with the emergence of Japan as a major player in the market place. Thus, with one assumes a heavy heart, Dennis left an industry which had been his life for almost 30 years.

However, his engineering talents did not go to waste and in 1970 D.G. Steel & Son was created.

This was not precisely true, as the business began its life as K Tex Engineering (reflecting its origins) - only changing its name to the current one in 1977 with the arrival of Tony Steel (The Son!)

Following its humble beginnings in small lean-to premises loaned to him by a friend in Heywood (just up the road!), Dennis expanded the business using the network of contacts he had built up during his time in the textile machinery business.

Between 1970 and 1977 the company bought its own premises (a compact 2,500 square feet), which were doubled by an extension in 1975 - the company by now employing 7/8 people, still very much serving the textile sector .

By the time 1977 arrived the continuing decline of Lancashire textiles and a fragile UK economy saw some difficult times and the arrival of Tony Steel (Ex-Dental Student) - another mouth for the company to feed !

However, due to a certain amount of good fortune Tony saw, or hoped he saw, a market opportunity in the manufacturing of gears and related toothed products - an area which had been exploited to a small degree in the company's textile past .

Above: Founder, Dennis Steel. **Left:** *The company's original premises in 1983.***Below:** *A bird's eye view of the companys Barnbrook Gear Works in Brook Street.*

Its premises now double the size of those in Heywood, the company was able to increase the size of work it was able to offer - increasing the maximum gear component size to some 3 metres diameter and maximum single component weight to 15 tons.

By the turn of the Millennium the company's workforce was now almost 30 and it had become a fairly large player in the 'Gear Market' in the UK.

Although the company had been steady during the 'noughties', like the decline of the Lancashire textile market before it, the erosion of the UK engineering market continued during the first decade of the new century.

By 1980 the company had all but left its textile heritage behind and was expanding in the 'Gear Business'. In 1982 the Moss Gear Company at Accrington was bought from the Receiver. This doubled the then modest turnover and in 1983 the company won the contract to supply all gear parts required by the Jones Cranes Company of Letchworth, this once again doubling the then not quite so modest turnover.

Throughout the recession of the early 1980s the company continued to expand and in fact was helped considerably by the demise of several large competitors, thus enabling the still small company to obtain machinery at attractive prices as these larger firms went under the hammer .

1985 saw a further extension to the premises and in 1987, with nowhere else to go, the purchase of additional premises, increasing the floorspace to some 11,000 square feet with 20 employees.

1987 saw a huge investment for the time (£100,000!) in 'Gear Grinding' equipment giving the company access to new markets and by 1989 with a final extension at the Heywood sites the company had grown as far as it could in Heywood.

Sadly, 1992 saw the death of Dennis Steel after a short illness, at the age of 70, having been in semi-retirement since 1985.

The early 90s further saw the company move forward with the purchase of another small competitor - J.& J. Industrial Ltd. and, of course, the move to Bury .

In 1994 the company concluded the purchase of the former premises of R.Lord & Son, a boiler maker whose business had been on the Barnbrook Boiler Works site in Brook Street since 1841.

The company again had to broaden its horizons and during the 2008 economic crisis the company began negotiations with a Global manufacturer of construction equipment and by January 2009 had an exclusive contract to supply gears for the largest sizes of their stone crusher range - a contract potentially worth some 1,000,000 euros - however, since the recession was still at its height this was initially somewhat of an academic achievement.

As previously mentioned, the economic crisis of 2008 and 2009 whilst obviously a difficult and worrying time, did much to focus the mind on the future direction of the company. Traditionally, as a small 'jobbing' gear manufacturer, the company's machinery was of the old conventional type, based on simple mechanical, hydraulic and electrical control systems. It was clear that the world was changing and D.G. Steel & Son would have to change or be left behind.

Top left: *Large Bevel Gear for steel rolling mill machinery.*
Below: *Assembly of Mill Pinion for Zinc/Lead Mine.*

With this in mind, the company embarked on a long-term investment in CNC (computer controlled) machinery. This meant that the still reliable and high quality equipment from the 1950s and 1960s would not be scrapped but would work alongside the new state-of-the-art machinery to propel the business forward.

Although investment in a time of recession may be perceived as a risky strategy, this did prove to be successful.

Since growth by acquisition has always been part of the company ethos, when the opportunity came to buy W.R. Anderton (an industrial clutch manufacturer in Castleton, Rochdale) this was seized with enthusiasm. The Anderton business proved to be an ideal 'bolt-on', dovetailing perfectly into the existing product range and providing a valuable additional source of income during the difficult days of 2009 and early 2010.

Times improved considerably during 2010 and 2011, seeing the company expand particularly in terms of overseas business, boosting exports from just 5% in 2007 to almost 65% in November 2011.

This provided the confidence for the company to expand again and move into a further 10,000 sq.ft. workshop in Porritt Street, close to the Brook Street works.

Once again it was clear that there was an obvious need for further investment in order keep pace with the increasing demand created by the world market - particularly the huge developing areas of China, Russia, India and Brazil. The additional new premises in Porritt Street gave the company the necessary extra space for the new equipment which was essential for expansion. Therefore, in early 2011 several new CNC machines were purchased to increase capacity for

'general machining' - this is basically producing components prior to the machining of the gear teeth. This done, it became increasingly apparent that having speeded up the manufacturing process prior to gear cutting, it was now the gear cutting process itself that had to be revolutionised.

The company looked to the USA to provide this new equipment and in April 2011 R.P. Machines in Statesville, North Carolina, were commissioned to build a very specialised machine tool to provide the solution to the bottleneck in gear cutting.

In October 2011 the $500,000 Gould & Eberhardt 60S gear

Top Left: Conventional machining of a bevel gear on a vertical boring machine. Above: Gear cutting of a 3 metre internal gear for Nickel Mine winding gear. Left: Final measurement of an internal helical gear for use in can making machinery.

It is in this area that the company sees the future and it is hoped that 2012 will see D.G. Steel & Son move forward into this 'Brave New World'.

Now operating on two sites in Bury, with a total of 32,000 sq.ft. and 35 employees (many of whom have been with the company for in excess of 20 years), it is a far cry from its humble lean-to beginnings - but in truth it is just a continuation of the vision and determination of a fine man and engineer - Dennis Steel.

gashing machine (one of only two in the world) was delivered and installed, thus, delivering massive improvements in gear machining times.

Now, with an additional investment of over £1,000,000 at the new premises, it is hoped that the business will be 'set fair' for the future.

Looking forward to 2012 and beyond, the company is again looking at cutting edge technology in its efforts to stay in the vanguard of gear manufacturing. The future will see the company, whilst not abandoning its traditional methods and machinery, explore the very frontiers of gear production. New developments in gear manufacturing are pointing to a future where gears historically made on specific 'gear machines' can now be produced on 'non-dedicated' CNC machining centres.

Top Left: *Tony Steel pictured with Gear Shop Foreman Nick Goodhew during the cutting of a 208 tooth gear - at 148 inches (almost 4 metres diameter) the largest gear ever cut (to date) at D.G. Steel.* **Above:** *The new Gould & Eberhardt 60S CNC gear gasher, installed in October 2011.* **Below:** *The D.G. Steel team in 2011.*

McKenzie-Martin - An Excellent Opening

Established in 1966, McKenzie-Martin Limited specialises in the design and manufacture of louvre systems, ventilation units, smoke ventilators and rooflights.

For almost half a century McKenzie-Martin, based at its Eton Hill Works, in Radcliffe, has been successfully supplying innovative, well produced and reliable ventilation products.

The widespread range now includes all manner of natural and powered roof ventilators and wall louvres together with rooflights, stairwell ventilators, smoke ventilators and extract fans. The range is further complimented by a number of industrial, commercial and architectural ventilation and screening louvre systems to meet every requirement. The product range has been refined over these many years by means of experience and product development backed by extensive evaluation and independent laboratory and wind tunnel testing.

These products form part of a comprehensive and well-established range manufactured to suit a wide variety of commercial, industrial and domestic applications.

Today the firm remains a family run business with long serving, knowledgeable and loyal staff committed to producing a high level of service and quality products.

The company founder was James 'Mac' Mckenzie Martin Waite. After being demobbed from the RAF at the end of the war he joined Robertson Thane Ltd (later known as H.H.Robertson), a major manufacturer of roofing materials and was based in its Ventilation Department. After leaving that company Mac pursued a career in the industrial roofing industry working for Industrial Engineering Ltd later known as Kelsey Roofing Industries, the country's largest roofing contractors at the time.

Top left: *Founder, James 'Mac' Mckenzie Martin Waite.* **Above:** *The original workshop at Albert Works in 1967.* **Below:** *The company premises pictured in 1980.*

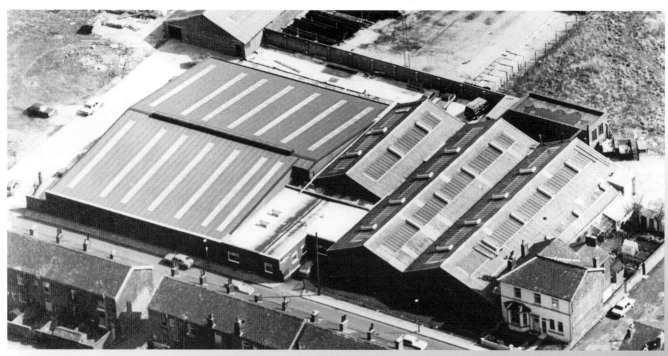

In early 1962 Mac established his own roofing contracting business known as Roofing Services Ltd, with branches across the UK, but he always had an ambition to establish his own ventilation company.

Whilst undertaking a particular roofing contract Mac showed his customer a ventilator design which the customer promptly ordered. Mac Waite quickly established a workshop and acquired sheet metal machinery in the Albert Works premises he had recently acquired and Mckenzie Martin Ltd was born. Harold Marcroft a skilled sheet metal foreman was the first employee, working for the firm until his retirement in 1993.

Mac employed a number of salesmen to promote the business, all of whom however, fell sadly short of the mark. In 1969 he was about to close the business when he mentioned to a friend and golfing partner John 'Jack' Booth his problems at Mckenzie Martin.

Jack Booth was looking for a career change and put himself forward as the answer to Mac Waite's problems. From then onwards, under Jack's direction, the company prospered and became very successful. Jack was new to ventilation, but he did

have some relevant experience. He had an engineering background and had been an apprentice draughtsman at Radcliffe Paper Mill. He had also had some business and sales experience.

Jack had to drive hundreds of miles each week to win customers for the small Radcliffe firm. By then McKenzie-Martin had been going for three years, had a labour force of just two, and was losing money.

Growth did come however, but not without a lot of hard work. Within a few short years the company was employing 20 people producing ventilators for industrial buildings in the firm's Albert Street works, off Water Street.

Although all the design of the firm's ventilators and louvres were similar, jobs were diverse because each factory roof is different and customers' requirements varied so much.

Top left: Sid Ratcliffe and Jack Hutchinson. ***Top right:*** *Pictured in 1987 are, from left to right: Harry Livingstone, Harold Marcroft, Jack Booth and Derek Edge.* ***Left:*** *McKenzie-Martin ventilation products.* ***Bottom left:*** *A sign of sucess in 1975 as Jack Booth is picture with a new company Volvo, fitted with private number plate.* ***Below:*** *One of the 16-metre high runs of McKenzie-Martin fixed blade louvres on the plant room tower at the University of Glasgow, 1990.*

With Jack's enthusiasm the firm began to look at export markets, and it soon had enquiries from as far away as Bolivia, Bahrain and Holland.

The company outgrew its premises at Albert Works and larger premises at Eton Hill Works on Eton Hill Road, in Radcliffe, were acquired.

Following the move to the new premises in 1978 the board of McKenzie-Martin was strengthened by the arrival of Derek Edge, who became the company's Commercial Director. The board at that time included Mac Waite, Jack Booth, Derek Edge and Harold Marcroft as well as Malcolm Whitehead who also acted as company secretary and accountant. In 1986 Jack Booth left the company and Harry Livingstone who had joined the company from Scotland became Sales Director. Harry would stay with the firm until his retirement in 2009.

stadium and Leigh Sports Village, not to mention the premises of many of the country's top companies and industries. The products are manufactured in a range of materials including sheet and extruded aluminium, plastic coated steel and powder coated steel and aluminium.

The current sales team is Mike Howard and David Ellis. Roy Bell is the longest serving member of the company who joined in 1969 and still works part-time in Product Development. In recent years Roy has been involved with most of the company's new product lines.

Tom Wagstaff was another long-seving member of McKenzie-Martin. Tom started in 1970 as Workshop Foreman and went on to become Production Controller. He retired in 2008 after 38 years with the company.

In 1988 Derek Edge sadly died after a short illness and was replaced by Tony Heap. Malcolm Whitehead also left the company in 1988, and Mac Waite's son Gordon Waite became Managing Director. Tony Heap left the company in 1997 to join his father's company. That same year saw Mark Pearse join the company as Production Director. Under Mark Pearse the manufacturing processes were completely overhauled and became increasingly computerised and automated. Mark has been responsible for promoting the company's move into offering fabrication components to industrial customers.

The company has supplied products around the globe including Europe, Africa, the Middle East and even the Falkland Islands. McKenzie-Martin products have been incorporated in many sporting venues including Manchester United's Old Trafford

*Top left: Mac Waite presents Harold Marcroft with gold carriage clock retirement gift in 1993. **Top right:** Gordon Waite (front) and the McKenzie-Martin staff pictured on the company's 25th anniversary in 1991. **Above:** Roy Bell. **Left:** McKenzie-Martin continuous Ventura rooflights. **Below:** A recent project of McKenzie-Martin was to supply their louvre systems to Stoke City's Britannia Stadium.*

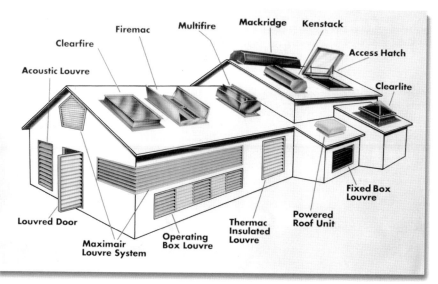

The long-serving and dedicated workforce is meeting future challenges with the same approach that has been successful since the company was founded - offering quality products, on time, and at sensible prices.

The company has many long-serving members of staff including Joe Brooks, Tony Brooks, Donald Sutterby, Andy Howard, Tim Buckley, Craig Anson, Nigel Parker, Nigel Kay, Phil Kay, Michael Weaver, Paul Gee, Matthew Milne and Chris Kirrane, company accountant.

Although McKenzie-Martin's original products were ridge and slope mounted ventilators, fixed and operated louvres and roofing flashings, the product range has constantly evolved. Over the years it has increased in size and range to include fire and smoke ventilators, Rooflights, Acoustic Louvres, Architectural Louvres and Fans as well as many other fabricated items and the Filuma sectional garage door range.

Product development has always been a vital concern to the company. Existing products are evaluated and improved on an ongoing basis.

Independent product testing for performance and fire rating has been undertaken by BSRIA (Building Services Research Information Association), Salford University's Department of Aeronautical and Mechanical Engineering and the Warrington Fire Research Centre Ltd.

Everything is made to meet bespoke requirements of a particular building design, and everything leaving the factory having to be 'right first time'.

Meanwhile, as markets have changed, a quarter of the company's output is now of items fabricated for clients within the engineering industry.

Today, led by Gordon Waite the founder's son, the firm is proud of its heritage, proud to be a family firm, and proud to be contributing to the ongoing story of the Bury area's long and distinguished industrial history.

Top left and left: Top left is a labelled diagram of McKenzie-Martin products and left is a more detailed view of a selection of those products: a Kenstack Ventilator (top left), Maximair Double Bank louvres, (bottom left), 'K' Series architectural louvre range (top centre) Ventura rooflights (bottom centre) and a Thermac Operating Louvre (right). **Top right:** Plant room louvres fitted on the Art & Design block at Suffolk College, Ipswich. **Below:** Managing Director, Gordon Waite (front centre) and some of the McKenzie-Martin team, 2011.

Radcliffe Glass & Windows - In the Frame

Today, double-glazed windows in our homes are the norm. One of the first local firms to offer double-glazing was Radcliffe Glass & Windows Ltd, a company now based in Lodge Road, Radcliffe.

Radcliffe Glass was established in Mellor Street, Radcliffe, in 1979 by local joiner Peter Andrew Turner and his wife Iris.

The firm began by doing simple glazing work and cutting glass to size. In 1985 the firm became the first double-glazing unit manufacturer in the area. With little competition the business flourished and a move to Lodge Brow followed in 1992.

However, after 20 years of trading in 1999 Peter Turner invited Steven Ainsworth, who had been with the company since 1987, to buy the firm as he was now ready for retirement. Steven's wife Susan mentioned the offer to her brother Clive Powers.

In February 2001, after very much deliberation, Clive joined Steven in becoming the new owners of Radcliffe Glass - though altering the name to Radcliffe Glass and Windows to mark their wider ambitions. Clive had come from a sales and marketing background working for large companies such as the Bank of

Scotland and General Electric. Clive's knowledge of marketing and administration coupled with Steven's wealth of experience of glass and glazing soon began to make a positive impact on the business. Within three weeks 'Fair Trades' membership had been applied for. Within six months cutting-edge glass-processing machinery had been bought, as well as introducing higher specification window frames. More UPVC window and door installations were made, despite stiff competition, whilst some of the larger kitchen and bathroom companies began to use the firm again.

Clive's wife, Kelly-Marie, who did all of the book-keeping during the first 18 months, soon found herself with plenty to keep count of. In the first year turnover had increased by more than 200 per cent, and an extra glass-cutter had to be taken on. In the second year another window-fitter was employed to help with larger installations. New lines were introduced such as 'Rosewood' a superior wood-effect PVC. With this great success in the UPVC window replacement field under their belt, Radcliffe Glass & Windows decided to branch out into the Conservatory and Orangery market.

In the second year turnover had again increased by more than 200 per cent. The third year of trading began with not only an increasing volume of installations but also with commissions from high profile customers such as The Bolholt Country Park Hotel, Polyflor, Harwood Golf Club and Bury Grammar School for Girls.

The growing business now became a limited company. Two new vans were fitted with the latest specification in racks for transporting glass. Another window-installer was employed to

Top: An aerial view of Radcliffe Glass, Circa 1970s. *Above: Early Radcliffe Glass advertising. **Left:** Radcliffe Glass & Windows' new Lodge Road premises, 2011. **Below:** Part of the Orangery range at Radcliffe Glass & Windows.*

2010 saw the firm become a founding member of the Double Glazing Ombudsman Scheme; the prestigious independent regulatory body for the double-glazing and conservatory industry. Over 67% of companies that apply for membership are refused and standards are monitored regularly. To add to the long list of accreditations, the company also became a registered Planitherm installer and part of the Planitherm network establishing the company as the number one A' rated window supplier in the area.

Not one to stand still, despite the fantastic achievements made in recent years, the firm recently did another full refurbishment of the showroom to showcase their Bi-Folding doors and Orangery range, alongside the Conservatory Display and house fronts.

provide two installation teams, whilst an office manager had to be taken on to cope with the new volume.

At Lodge Brow the rear of the building was opened up to provide a showroom and office as well as a trade counter.

In 2004 the firm celebrated 25 years in the glass business, which is no mean feat. Turnover had reached a staggering £1 million, with the bulk of new sales coming from customer recommendations.

In 2007 Clive Powers became sole Director of Radcliffe Glass & Windows Ltd after buying Steven out. Some seven months later the company moved to much larger premises a stone's throw away in Lodge Road. The new premises were completely refurbished, including a large showroom which is unrivalled in the area. Radcliffe Glass & Windows then moved into the commercial market, installing windows and doors for the entire Radcliffe Swimming Baths and Bury Castle Leisure Centre. The product range also widened to include Aluminium and Timber along with the UPVC.

In 2009 the firm became well-known for its sponsorship of local professional Boxer and British Title Holder Scott Quigg and also World Champion Thai boxer Andy Thrasher.

Despite the current recession, a very proud Clive and Kelly have seen Radcliffe Glass & Windows' turnover increase year on year resulting in additional land being bought for further expansion.

There is no question that Radcliffe Glass & Windows still has the latest technologically advanced products in comparison to their competitors and prides itself in staying ahead of the competition.

Meanwhile, in 2011, a sister company, Your Energy Specialists Ltd, was formed which specialises in PV Solar Panels. The first installation of panels went into Radcliffe Glass & Windows' own premises to help reduce the company's carbon footprint and electricity bills. Another bold step for the Radcliffe Glass & Windows Directors in which the success achieved so far can hopefully be repeated with the sister company.

Top left: Clive and Kelly-Marie pictured after the opening of the new showroom in 2007. **Bottom left:** One of the firm recent conservatory installations. **Above:** Bi-Folding doors. **Below:** Clive Powers, Managing Director, 2011.

Bury Van Group - Hire and Hire

Bury Van Group is one of the largest privately owned vehicle hire companies in the North West. The business is based at Limefield House, Limefield Brow, once home to the Ashton family, prominent local manufacturers in the 19th century.

What today is the Bury Van Hire Group was born out of coincidence, enthusiasm and opportunity.

Roy Cole, the company founder, and still its Chief Executive, had spent his formative years in the construction industry. He was instrumental in planning the footprint, layout and construction of the first two nuclear power stations in the UK, in Essex and Wales.

By 1973 one of Roy's colleagues had formed a plant hire and construction company with the grand total of just one asset – a single JCB.

Roy and his colleague saw the opportunity to expand into the plant hire business and Roy was persuaded give up his job at Balfour Beatty to join forces to focus full-time on developing a viable long term operation.

The first few years proved eventful. Firstly, Roy's business partner felt the full impact of Cupid's arrow after meeting an Irish lady and left the business to permanently settle on the Emerald Isle. Secondly, the recession of the 1970s hit hard, and James E Turner, where Roy had his base, went into receivership.

Above: A bird's eye view of Bury Van Group's Limefield House, Limefield Brow, premises. Left: A company Fiesta from 1979. Below: An early company vehicle decked out as a float for the local gala in the 1980s.

By the 1970s Roy was working for Balfour Beatty, one of the longest established construction companies in England, as Senior Site Manager in the North West.

In order to establish a business base in the North West, Roy Cole established a relationship with another long-established civil engineering company, James E. Turner Ltd, and rented out 'The Lodge', the old gatehouse to Limefield House.

Undaunted, and with dogged determination, Roy was loathe to see his hard work wasted. In 1980 he bought the whole of the site from the receivers, which meant that he had a larger base to use. This sowed the seeds of a strategy to expand the business by moving into hiring commercial vehicles as well as hiring out plant.

Sub-dividing the old Turner's site and leasing parts of it to tenants obtained funding to grow the still-nascent Bury Van Group. Over time this made possible some diversification, away from hiring out excavators and diggers to hiring out small vans and cars.

The economic recovery of the early 1980s saw steady growth, and by the mid-eighties Bury Van Group had two new recruits: a cat called Henry, who just wandered in one day and decided to stay, and a young Yvonne Wilkinson.

Yvonne is now a Director of Bury Vehicle Leasing, and General Manger of long- term Contract Hires. She says today's group of companies is a far cry from when she started, with just two staff members, very long hours and the need to be a jack-of-all trades. She attributes the slow gentle growth over a long period to being "polite, prompt and professional".

Henry the cat is, unfortunately, no longer with the company.

By the turn of the 21st century the growing Bury Van Group required increasing levels of expertise and professionalism. Roy recruited the current Managing Director, Martin Connaughton, and current Sales Manager, Dave McCoy, both from Hertz Rent a Car.

Additionally, the current depot manager Rick Brace has worked his way up from joining as a car cleaner to running the Customer Hire Desk as Depot Manager.

The larger team's abilities and expertise enabled Bury Van Group to develop further and expand into hiring a broad range of vehicles including, among others, Hire Cars, Ford Transit Vans, Pick-Up Trucks, Minibuses, 7.5 Tonne Sleeper Vans and 44 Tonne Tractor Units.

Roy also bought Castlecroft Garage in Bury in order to service and maintain the ever-expanding fleet of vehicles now owned by the Bury Van Group, as well as providing a traditional MOT and repair service to the general public.

Roy Cole, now in his mid-seventies, has been developing the business for four decades. Today he and his wife Brigid spend their time between their home in Surrey and the operation in Bury.

Is Roy ready get out of the driving seat at Bury Van Hire and get into the back seat? Don't bet on it!

This page: Examples of the wide selection of vehicles available for hire from Bury Van Group.

J&W Whewell Ltd
A New Chapter

J&W Whewell Ltd's New Bridge Chemical Works, in York Street, Radcliffe, has been a familiar sight to generations during the course of more than a century. Today, the long-established firm is led by brothers John and Mark Walker.

The firm was founded in 1880, also by two brothers, Joseph and William Whewell. They specialised in producing resin size and oils. Their New Bridge works premises were soon extended to incorporate the adjoining Lloyds textile mill.

A second generation of Whewells, also named William and Joseph, followed on in the business, taking over from their fathers.

Throughout their lives, in addition to their chemical commitments, both of the second generation brothers were fanatically interested in horses. William devoted his life to shire horses and consistently produced show-winning specimens from his Heaton Grove stud in Manchester Road.

William's daughter, Gene, and son, Joseph Whewell, were joined later by the next generation, Joseph III's son William. Joseph Whewell III started a bulk haulage company. The transport company was bought out by Joseph and his son William and relocated.

J&W Whewell Ltd was now bought by Gene Whewell. The small chemical company was on the verge of bankruptcy. Lack of investment over many years meant that a major injection of capital was required in the late 1990s, a time which unfortunately coincided with a significant downturn in business.

Happily, those problems were overcome. With some 25 employees the company marketed its products in the United Kingdom to many industries, including textiles, lubricants, surfactants formulators, and the paper and printing trade. Abroad, disinfectant, leather and oils manufacturers were keen to buy from Whewells.

Astonishingly, J&W Whewell Ltd makes over 300 different products: leather chemicals, textile auxiliaries, sulphated chemicals and oils, phosphate esters, sulphosuccinates and soaps. A multi-purpose plant allows the company to manufacture all these different types of chemicals on site. The firm is one of only two manufacturers of sulphated oils and chemicals in the United Kingdom. Best of all, from a customer's point of view, is that being multi-skilled and of a modest size the company is flexible enough to offer tailor-made products for their specific needs.

Top left: Joseph Whewell, co-founder of J&W Whewell. *Above:* William Whewell, father of Gene Whewell, who at one time had up to 30 shire horses at his Heaton Grove stud. *Left:* Gene Whewell pictured outside the company's New Bridge Chemical Works in 2004.

J&W Whewell Ltd was acquired by brothers John and Mark Walker in 2009. Back in 1990, they had started making bleach and washing-up liquid in a small shed on a farm in Heywood. They began manufacturing their products with the most basic equipment. They sold their products door to door. As they made money they bought more and better equipment.

Progress was not, however, all plain sailing. It was very difficult for a small firm to keep abreast of evermore demanding Health and Safety and chemical legislation. These days it's a full-time job for one of the firm's team.

Now more than twenty years on, with some forty staff, the Walker brothers' products are sold all over the United Kingdom, from market stalls to supermarkets, packaged to suit individual clients' needs.

The acquisition of J&W Whewell by the Walker brothers was a great step forward. They had known Gene Whewell for all the years they had been in business. She had always been helpful and supportive towards them. When Gene decided to retire they had no hesitation in offering to take up the reins. As the brothers say, "Whewells is a wonderful business, one of Bury's oldest, with a fantastic history and reputation. We are honoured to take the company forward."

The acquisition has given the Walker brothers the leading edge in their industry, producing raw materials to complement their existing packaging and labelling, completing the chain of production, and enabling them to combine quality products with the best prices and the best possible service.

Meanwhile the Walker brothers didn't do it all on their own. As the brothers say: "We owe an immense debt of gratitude to all our families and friends for all their help and support over more than two decades. Without them it would have taken longer to get where we are today. A big sincere thank you for all your help."

Above: John (right) and Mark Walker outside J&W Whewell's New Bridge Chemical Works, 2011. *Below:* One of three production plants inside the works.

Senior Hargreaves

A Pioneer in Creating Better Environments

In 1872 Henry Hargreaves, a time-served tinsmith, was established with his father making baking tins and grass boxes in a workshop in the Heywood Street/Cook Street area of Bury. By 1892 the company had acquired retail premises in Silver Street from where they traded as general ironmongers and bicycle assemblers. From 1890 this business began manufacturing ornate turret roof ventilators in tin and copper. Many of these were used on churches, schools, factories and theatres throughout the area.

In the 1950s the company began the manufacture of ductwork for heating ventilation and air-conditioning. The first major contract, lasting for five years, and with a value of £500,000, was for the Shell Building in London, in 1957. Hargreaves ductwork was also used in the Concorde development programme. A full scale prototype was alternately blasted with hot and cold air to simulate the heating and cooling that would take place during supersonic flight and so predict the long term effect of expansion and contraction on the aircraft structure.

In 1957 the Senior Engineering Company took a partial shareholding in the company. The Senior interest was extended to a total takeover in 1963 and the tie with the Hargreaves family was broken after more than 90 years. Senior Hargreaves continues to be a business unit within the publicly quoted company, Senior Plc.

Many significant buildings, including The Barbican Centre, NatWest Tower, London City Hall and Portcullis House, all feature Hargreaves ductwork and ventilation equipment. In Richard Rogers' iconic Lloyds Building, the Hargreaves stainless steel ductwork is a building feature, hung on the outside of the structure to maximise the available space within the building.

Over a 30-year period the company has been involved in significant industrial projects, not least at Sellafield in Cumbria. These include the thermal oxide reprocessing plant (THORP), the advanced gas-cooled reactor (ACR) decommissioning and, from 2009, the separation area ventilation (SAV) project.

Recently Hargreaves has become involved with major transport infrastructure projects. Three tunnels on High Speed One, the channel tunnel rail link, use Hargreaves ventilation on both the deep tunnels and the Thames Tunnel.

The Thames tunnels are fitted with Saccardo nozzles at the portals to introduce air at high volume and velocity into the access and evacuation tunnel if there is an emergency. This is a particular area of Hargreaves expertise and Saccardo nozzles by Hargreaves are also used in the Holmesdale and Bell Common tunnels on the M25.

Fire engineering is a significant part of the company business. Hargreaves Fire Duct (HFD) is a product engineered to resist fire and provide a means for the safe removal of smoke and the dangerous products of combustion from within buildings. HFD products meet regulatory requirements for stability, integrity and insulation and so safeguard life, protect property and improve the chances that an enterprise affected by fire will survive and recover.

Many venues for sport and entertainment are ventilated by Hargreaves. This includes hospitality suites at Wimbledon, Wembley Stadium, Manchester Arena, Reebok Stadium, Wilkinson Eyer's Liverpool Echo Arena and BT Conference Centre located on the waterfront near to Albert Dock.

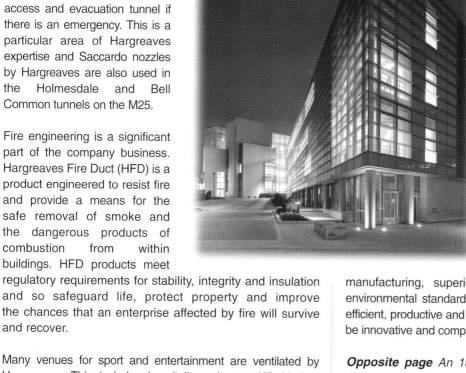

In addition to major contract works, the company also plays a significant role in the heating and ventilation industry via its nationwide network of trade outlets, Ductshops. Each location carries large stocks of ductwork, fans, grilles and accessories making quality product accessible on competitive terms to local contractors undertaking smaller scale projects.

Hargreaves has a stable and dedicated workforce, many of who started at the company as apprentices. This know-how is a major business asset and one that the company continues to cultivate with a modern apprentice programme.

The company still operates from premises at the junction of Cook Street and Lord Street and remains one of the largest private sector employers in Bury. Modernisation has seen the introduction of lean manufacturing, superior quality systems and enhanced environmental standards. This has made the company more efficient, productive and sustainable and confident that they will be innovative and competitive for the next 140 years.

Opposite page An 1890s view of Henry Hargreaves' 32 Silver Street premises. ***Above and below:*** *Two of Senior Hargreaves' recent projects: The AstaraZeneca (above), an advanced pharmaceutical research building in Cheshire, and the Liverpool Arena which was designed by Wilkinson Eyre, a leading international architectural practice.*

ACKNOWLEDGMENTS

The publishers would like to sincerely thank a number of individuals and organisations
for their help and contribution to this publication.

John Jeffay (Cascade News) - Bury Times

Ken Potter (HPAC) - Bury Image Bank

NOSTALGIC BURY

'Sweet sweet the memories you gave to me', so sang Dean Martin in his famous recording of 1956. When you read 'Nostalgic Bury' you will be transported back to that era and beyond. We make no apologies for taking a backward glance and allowing the reader to wallow a little in the glow of nostalgia. They are the years in which we grew up and our parents and grandparents made their way through life.

As part of the 'Memories' series of books it is a rare collection of photographs that will awaken half forgotten thoughts of yesteryear and confirm descriptions of life that the older generation told us about. Carefully researched text, adding depth and interest, enhances each image. Sometimes the writing is factual, elsewhere it is wry but in every case it gives the reader a flavour of how life used to be.

Collectively these images capture the essence of what local life was like from the turn of the last century. Above all, these photographs and captions are intended to bring back nostalgic memories of how things were in a time that seems like only yesterday...

ISBN 978-1906649722

www.truenorthbooks.com